Finding Your Inner Moose

Also from Islandport Press

The Sweet Life
Ida LeClair's Guide to Love and Marriage
By Susan Poulin

John McDonald's Maine Trivia
By John McDonald, with illustrations by Mark Ricketts

Down the Road a Piece: A Storyteller's Guide to Maine
By John McDonald

Bert and I . . . The Book
By Marshall Dodge and Robert Bryan

Headin' for the Rhubarb!
A New Hamsphire Dictionary (well, kinda)
By Rebecca Rule

Live Free and Eat Pie!
A Storyteller's Guide to New Hampshire
By Rebecca Rule

Not Too Awful Bad: A Storyteller's Guide to Vermont
By Leon Thompson

Finding Your Inner Moose

Ida LeClair's Guide to Livin' the Good Life

Susan Poulin

ISLANDPORT PRESS

Islandport Press, Inc.
P.O. Box 10
Yarmouth, Maine 04096
www.islandportpress.com
info@islandportpress.com

ISBN: 978-1-944762-93-3
Library of Congress Card Number: 2012934446
Printed in USA

Dean L. Lunt, publisher
Teresa Lagrange, cover design

To my parents, Betty and Pat, and my sister, Jane. Your sense of humor; good, old-fashioned common sense; and joie de vivre infuse Ida's world and serve as the foundation for my life. What a gift.

To Gordon Carlisle, my friend, husband, and creative partner. Thank you for so lovingly keeping Ida sounding like Ida. You continue to inspire me with your ferocious talent.

Table of Contents

Foreword

by Rebecca Rule

Meet Ida LeClair, who—along with best friends Celeste, Rita, Betty, Dot, and Shirley—make up the social club Women Who Run with the Moose. They considered calling themselves Women Who Run with the Potatoes and Women Who Crawl with the Lobsters, but potatoes and lobsters, though powerful totems, didn't carry the cachet of a moose.

Ida LeClair is, in turn, the creation and alter ego of Susan Poulin, writer, actress, storyteller, and all-around talented, lively, warm, funny, and highly original human being. She wrote this book. She writes Ida. She kind of is Ida, but not really—if you catch my drift.

Ida cashiers down to the A&P. She enjoys it. She enjoys her customers. Most of them. She's determined to enjoy most things in life. That's just the way she is. She certainly enjoys the Women Who Run with the Moose, and chronicles their adventures as they shop, get their hair done, eat out, diet, play practical jokes on their husbands, take day trips to the big cities (Portland and Bangor), and, generally, squeeze as much juice out of life in Mahoosuc Mills, Maine, as there is to squeeze. The girls have a darned good time. And, God, don't they like to laugh! And don't they find a lot to laugh about.

Not the least of which is their husbands. Ida loves her Charlie to death, it's true, but that doesn't blind her to some of his idio-syncrasies. Or her own. As she and the girls age, as gracefully as possible, they are often inspired by, what else, the moose.

"The moose has a flap of skin under its chin called 'the bell,' " Ida explains, "which kind of sways as it walks. That didn't use to apply to me, but the older I get, ding-dong. What can you do?"

What you can do is take what comes in stride with an easy moose-like lope, always remembering to laugh.

So, here's what you'll find on these pages:

- Ida's stories of her life in Mahoosuc Mills.
- Ida's how-to-live-life-to-the-fullest advice gleaned from her experiences.
- Moose lore galore.
- Ida's husband Charlie's peanut-gallery observations, except they're not from the peanut gallery, they're from his beloved Barcalounger.
- Ida's niece Caitlin piping up now and then with her New Agey take on Ida's wisdom and, perhaps, offering a writing or breathing or imagining exercise to help you find your inner moose.
- Ida's down-to-earth (and hilarious) reinterpretation of Caitlin's instructions.

What you'll also find on these pages is a guide to living with few regrets, with integrity, and *joie de vivre* (that's French, like Ida). And you'll find moments of recognition (that's me!) along with many smiles, many belly laughs, and some wicked good advice.

Like: Whenever you find a restroom, use it; you never know when the next opportunity will present itself. Ida calls this theory *Carpe Peeum*.

Like: Whenever you find a restroom, use it; you never know when the next opportunity will present itself. Ida calls this theory Carpe Peeum.

Like: Pick one healthy thing you know you should be doing and get it over with early in the day.

Or: Nourish your friendships and yourself by having a standing breakfast or lunch date with a friend or two.

Something I learned: Moose calves are born with their eyes wide open—wide open! Ida LeClair's eyes are wide open.

And so is her heart.

Rebecca Rule is a storyteller and author. She regularly performs throughout New Hampshire, and her humor books include *Headin' for the Rhubarb! A New Hampshire Dictionary (well, kinda)* and *Live Free and Eat Pie! A Storyteller's Guide to New Hampshire*. She has also written the children's books, *The Iciest, Diciest, Scariest Sled Ride Ever!*, and *N is for New Hampshire*.

Author's Note

When did I meet Ida? 1996.

I was competing in the first (and, as far as I know, only) Yankee Yarns Contest in Keene, New Hampshire. At the contest, there were people from all over New England telling ten-minute stories in different categories: "traditional," "contemporary," "for children," etc.

I entered the contest on a lark to tell a story of mine called "The Stud Finder," which placed me squarely in the "contemporary" category. My story took a new look at an old problem—finding a guy. I didn't think I stood a chance. In fact, I secretly hoped the judges might give me an Honorable Mention for "most sexual innuendo in a Yankee Yarn." (Not a high bar since the genre is devoid of sexual innuendo.)

No one was more surprised than me when I actually won in my category and got to perform that night at the Colonial Theatre. Veteran Maine storyteller Tim Sample was the host that evening. He and Bob Bryan of "Bert and I" fame told some of the old "Bert and I" stories that Bob and Marshall Dodge had made famous.

So, I was in good company. But as the show progressed, I realized that I was the only woman on stage, flanked by a bunch of guys in flannel shirts joking about their mothers-in-law. I listened to them and thought, "You know what? These stories are okay, but they don't portray the strength, humor, and good old-fashioned common sense of the women I knew growing up." Plus, their point of view reflected a Yankee sensibility (it was a

Yankee Yarns Contest, after all) that was a world away from the Franco-American culture in which I was raised, way up near the border of Québec. Where was the *joie de vivre*?

And that's when Ida came to me. I wanted to create a character who would pay homage to those women; a gal who didn't have much formal education, but who possessed a strong sense of herself, a great sense of humor, and "street smarts," if you can use such a term for someone who lives in a small town. Most importantly, I wanted to create a gal with a Franco-American background who spoke with a Maine accent, like so many in my family.

I clearly remember the exact moment it happened—the day she first appeared to me. One morning as I sat staring at my blank computer screen, I heard this voice in my head say, "Hi there! My name's Ida, and I'm a Home Shopping Networkaholic."

Voila! Ida was born.

I found I could naturally channel this wonderful and oh-so-familar woman. Ida told me stories even if I came to my computer empty. I saw my mother in her immediately, and my dad, and many of the wise and wonderful people I knew growing up. The more I wrote, the more a familiar world unfolded; a world quite apart from the one that appeared in traditional Down East stories.

Early on, I determined that Ida would not be a caricature. No, she'd be a three-dimensional person living in a small town in Western Maine. And although it might be hard to find Mahoosuc Mills on a map, the town is real to me, and it's filled with stories. I know I can open any door in Mahoosuc Mills and there is a story waiting. Ida works as a cashier down to the A&P, and stories walk into that store every day.

I am continually discovering new things about Ida and her world. Heck, I still discover new things about her in the orginal Ida play even though I've been performing it on and off for more than twenty years. I think that's because I know more about Ida now than I did when I wrote the play. I'm a different person now, so I've gained a different perspective.

Through Ida, I've had the opportunity to write in different forms—plays, blogs, and books. Each form stretches me in unique ways. The same story might appear on a blog, in a book, or as a play. Each version must be crafted in a slightly different way to fit the form. So Ida has made me a better writer.

Ida has also made me a better performer. She's such a big personality, I've had to expand my acting tools accommodate her energy. When you are the only person on stage, the audience is your scene partner. And I've found with Ida in my corner, I'm more daring. I'm no longer held hostage by the rules of theater. I can respond to a comment from the audience, and improvise on the spot. Ida can laugh at her own jokes. In short, I'm more relaxed, and I have more fun.

And then there's laugh surfing. When you're on stage, you learn pretty quickly that laugher is a lot like a wave. It builds and then it crests. If you have a two or three joke set-up (which happens a lot in Ida's world), you can't wait for the wave to completely dissipate before starting to talk again. If you do that, the show will lose momentum and the next joke will fall flat. As a performer, you must listen and time when you jump in for maximum lift off. I call it "laugh surfing," and Ida's pretty darn good at it.

When premiering a new Ida play, Ida makes me more fearless because while the show may be new, the character isn't—I'm not starting from zero. I can listen to the audience and hone the play from performance to performance during those first shows of the run. When I debuted Makin' Whoopie, for example, I cut about two pages between the first night and the next day's matinee. I flipped some jokes and changed the ending—no problem. I continued honing the show during the fall through twelve performances at three different venues until I got it where I wanted it.

In a strange way, Ida has been a mentor. When I'm in a some sort of jam I ask myself, "What would Ida do?" See, she has a different back-story than I do, so she experiences the world in a different way. She often sees solutions to problems that I don't. Ida helps me view things in my life from a different perspective.

I've learned a lot from Ida over the years. She gets me outside the box, creatively. She makes me laugh and sometimes even cry. After six plays, two books, and ten years of weekly blogs, Ida continues to surprise and intrigue me. I'm looking forward to she and I growing old together, and can't wait to see what new adventures will come our way.

—Susan

One

You Can Learn a Lot from a Moose

Hi there! My name's Ida LeClair. I live in Mahoosuc Mills, a small town in western Maine, with my husband, Charlie, and our little dog, Scamp.

Never heard of Mahoosuc Mills? Can't find it on a map? Well, it's true, we're not on a lot of maps. But trust me, we're there. You just have to know where to look. I suspect you may have even unknowingly visited our fine town, or at least one very similar; you might even live in one yourself.

I've lived here in Mahoosuc Mills my whole life. My husband, Charlie, too. We went to Moose Megantic High together. Now we live in a beautiful double-wide mobile home in town.

Charlie works at the mill, has worked there since graduation. He's a foreman now, and I'm a cashier down to Super Food World, though people in town still call it the A&P. I also moonlight doing books for Smitty's Hardware and the Mahoosuc Mills Mainely Maine store. My hobbies include country line dancing and making crafts, but my favorite is having adventures with my special group of best friends—Celeste, Rita, Betty, Dot, and Shirley. We call ourselves Women Who Run with the Moose.

I just love living in a small town—it gives you a real sense of community when you're greeted by name at the post office or down to the transfer station, and when everyone knows your business. Well, that last one not so much.

I was reminded just how much I like living here the other day when Rose Thibodeau got out of rehab—not your Betty Ford kind of rehab, rather the rehab wing of Mahoosuc Green, the senior living facility here in town.

Rose's children tried to get her to move into Mahoosuc Green permanent, but Rose wasn't budging—she's eighty-nine, still living at home, and aims to keep it that way. Well, a short while back she took a tumble, breaking one wrist and spraining the other. I don't know how long she was lying on the floor before her daughter, Claire, found her. Of her seven kids, only Claire and her brother, Noël, still live here in town, and one of them tries to check in on Rose every day.

So Rose was in rehab six weeks. I run into Claire at the Marching Band Boosters' Bake Sale a coupla weekends ago, and she told me they used this little setback of her mother's as an opportunity to do some negotiating. In order for Rose to come home, she had to agree to wear one of them Lifelines—that's the necklace with the button you push if you're in trouble, have fallen, or something like that.

One of the very first things Rose wanted to do after leaving rehab was come to the A&P. She never needs much. Rose gets Meals on Wheels for lunch while Claire and her sister-in-law, Ronnie, take turns bringing her supper. But Rose isn't really into it for the food. She likes coming to the A&P because she gets to drive around in our little motorized shopping cart. And God help anyone who gets in her way.

Now Rose was never that great a driver to begin with, always getting into little fender benders or nicking the curb. They finally took her license away four years ago. Rose was backing out of her garage and accidentally put her car in drive instead of reverse. She looked over her shoulder, stepped on the gas pedal, and smashed right through the back wall of her garage, taking out the clothesline and a week's worth of clean laundry, slamming into the picnic table, and stopping just inches from her Mary on a Half Shell statue.

Rose was stove up pretty bad, but somehow she managed to get out of the car, go into the house, and call Noël.

Rose told everyone, "The Virgin Mary saved me. It was a miracle!"

Needless to say, the sight of Rose Thibodeau behind the wheel of that motorized shopping cart the other day made more than one of us workers at the A&P get religion real quick. To be honest, she started out okay, going up and down the first couple of aisles nice and slow. I

> *Rose told everyone, "The Virgin Mary saved me. It was a miracle!"*

think she was still shaken up from her accident, but she got her confidence back pretty quick. Next thing you know, she sent a pyramid of navel oranges cascading across the produce section. Then she took out an end-of-aisle display of fruit cocktail, scaring the you-know-what out of little Donny Bragdon. Donny was in mid-tantrum because he wanted some Cheetos when Rose hit the fruit cocktail and was then bearing down on him full bore. Fortunately, Donny managed to leap behind his mother just as Rose went whizzing past. Donny was a complete angel for the rest of their shopping excursion.

But you know, as much of a pain in the neck it is to have Rose wreaking havoc in the store, it was nice to see her back in action. The A&P just wasn't the same without her terrorizing us once a week. Rose is part of Mahoosuc Mills, so we miss her when she's not around.

That's just how it is in a small town.

In a small town, you're thrown together with a group of people (let's be honest, some you like more than others), and you have to find a way to get along. You learn pretty quick that whether you like it or not, everybody knows your business. Small-town people have long memories, and the only way to avoid running into someone is never leaving your house.

On the flip side, if you're having a hard time, you know folks will rally 'round to lend you a hand. So small-town living helps you develop a sense of grace when it comes to dealing with people, or at the very least, some compassion for those who can't seem to get out of their own way. And because you're all connected, you have this desire to give back to the community. I wonder if it isn't like that where you live, too?

Mahoosuc Mills Is . . .

- A place with a wicked long winter, followed by two months of mud season, maybe a week of spring before the blackflies move in, a short summer (seems hotter than it used to be when I was a kid), and one glorious fall.
- Where some folks from away come on vacation, then instead of enjoying it, complain about how it's not like the place they're takin' a break from.
- My hometown.

The Women Who Run with the Moose

In Mahoosuc Mills I hang out with the greatest group of gals and, as I mentioned, we call ourselves Women Who Run with the Moose. I bet you're wondering how we got our name. Well, it must be twenty-five years ago now when me and my friends Celeste, Rita, Betty, Dot, and Shirley went to a "Women Who Run with the Wolves" study group down to the library. Oh, I tell you, that group was pretty much drop-dead serious! Lots of talking about being a wild woman, but not much doing it. Us girls couldn't even get them to come with us down to Portland to see the Chippendales!

After suffering through that study group session, we got inspired to form our own women's group, one that actually runs wild from time to time. Then we start talking about what we're going to call the group, right? Since we're all from Maine, we thought it should have something to do with our state.

"Women Who Run with the Potato" got voted down pretty quick. Likewise, we nixed "Women Who Crawl with the Lobster." Then it come to me: "Women Who Run with the Moose." And we all let out a whoop! It just felt right, you know?

Then we start sharing what we know about moose, which wasn't all that much at the time. First off, there are moose in Maine. Second, moose are wild. They're good-natured, independent, have a sharp sense of smell and excellent hearing. And they show up in the darnedest places. You know, people think moose are dumb, but they were smart enough to have a law passed to protect them.

Now, us girls just love to shop, so that night we beelined it to the Mahoosuc Mills Trading Post in search of moose paraphernalia.

5

We couldn't believe our eyes when we found a genuine mega-bugle bull-moose caller. That night I became the official keeper of the caller. I bring it every time the Women Who Run with the Moose get together.

God, we have a good time! Our feeling is, if you have fun doing something, even if it don't turn out exactly the way you planned, well, you know what? You've still had a good time.

A Certified Maine Life Guide

Anyhoo, I also recently became a Certified Maine Life Guide. I was going to call myself a "life coach," but let's face it, I don't look like any of the life coaches you see on TV—you just know those perky, pulled-together gals have a personal stylist, a personal trainer, and at least one college diploma tucked away in their fancy-schmancy office.

Life coaches tend to talk about "self care" and "vision boards," and all that can be a little too woo-woo for me. They have lots of good tools, of course, but some of 'em just aren't practical for people who work two jobs to pay the bills.

So one day, I'm watching this glammed-up life coach on the *The Today Show*. She's talking about going on a "vision quest" to find your "life path," and I'm thinking, "That just don't make sense. We're already on our life path, aren't we?" Sure, some of us may have wandered onto a side trail that's hard going at the moment, and we may need a little help getting back onto a less-rugged path, but this is it. This is our life, and we need to stop putting it under a microscope and start living it. And, here's a startlin' concept—maybe we should even have fun while we're doing it.

Being a life coach was out of the question, though. First off, there's the looks, not to mention the schooling. Besides, when I think of a coach, I picture Coach Murphy from Moose Megantic High. He was all about training hard and not taking no for an answer. No pain, no gain was his motto, which I must say is a motto that is hard to get really excited about.

But as I see it, life guiding's something altogether different. It's more like a gentle nudge in the right direction, lending a hand when someone needs a little help getting out of the puckerbrush and back on the trail. Besides, guiding runs in my family.

See, my grandfather, Frederick Gilbert, was a Registered Maine Guide. Folks from away would come up to Maine to go hunting or fishing, and they'd hire him to take them places they could never have found on their own. Story has it, Grampy Gilbert dropped out of school after third grade and came to Maine from Quebec in his teens. He spoke French, of course, and Frenchified English, or Franglais as we call it, but basically he was illiterate in both languages.

Back then you didn't have to pass a written test to be a Registered Maine Guide, which was a good thing for Grampy Gilbert. You just needed your local game warden to say you knew what you were doing. Being the outdoorsman that he was, Grampy Gilbert passed the test with flying colors. 'Course, it didn't hurt that his cousin was the game warden.

Grampy Gilbert loved the outdoors, and was blessed with an amazing internal compass and a special knack for showing people a good time. Plus, he just had the kind of good, old-fashioned common sense that you can't get from book learning. As a Maine guide, Grampy Gilbert's job was to take people where they wanted to go, make sure they had fun along the way, and help them get home again safe and sound. And that, in a nutshell, my friends, is what I'm aiming to do for you.

7

Now how, you may ask, did I get certified as a Maine Life Guide? Well, once I got the notion of doing this, I told a few people about my idea. Of course, quick as a wink everyone in town knew my plans. Then, one Saturday evening, I'm at the bean supper down to the Congo Church, trying to nab a slice of peanut butter pie before they're all gone, when Claudia Peavey (there's one in every town) marches up to me and says, "I heard you're calling yourself a Maine Life Guide now. What? You think you're going to be on the Oprah Network or something? You've had a lot of crazy ideas before, Ida, but this one takes the cake. You're certifiable!"

> *And as my husband, Charlie, is fond of saying, "Sweetheart, being a Life Guide is perfect for you. You just love giving advice to people, whether they ask for it or not!"*

And I'm thinking, you know what? She's right; I am. I am certifiable. Sometimes it takes a little bit of crazy to broaden your horizon. So that was that. I became a Certified Maine Life Guide.

Now, a little more about my credentials (for those of you who like to know that sort of thing). I may not have a bunch of degrees hanging on my wall, but I've worked as a cashier down to the A&P since I was seventeen, which means I know most everybody in Mahoosuc Mills, and then some. I am a daughter, a sister, an aunt, a wife, and a best friend, with almost sixty years of experience in the field. Plus, I like to think I've inherited at least a smidge of my Grampy Gilbert's common sense. And as my husband, Charlie, is fond of saying, "Sweetheart, being a Life Guide is perfect for you. You just love giving advice to people, whether they ask for it or not!"

"Fly Rod" Crosby

As a Certified Maine Life Guide, I feel I have a sister in "Fly Rod" Crosby, the first Registered Maine Guide. Yes indeed, the first Maine Guide was a woman, if you can believe that, way back in 1897. She started out working in a bank, but was kind of sickly. A doctor told her she needed to spend more time out of doors, so she moved to the Rangeley Lakes area. Turns out, his advice worked wonders for her.

Cornilia Thurza Crosby got her nickname when the outdoor articles she wrote started being published in a syndicated column called "Fly Rod's Journal." According to legend, she supposedly caught two hundred trout in one day and was the last person to legally kill a caribou buck in the state. Fly Rod also did a lot to promote Maine as a tourist destination for hunting and fishing. She had a booth at the first annual Sportsmen's Show in Madison Square Garden down to New York City. She stood there with her rifle and a fishing rod, and if that didn't get folks' attention, her green doeskin skirt that only came to just below her knees sure did. Scandalous!

I found this quote from Fly Rod on the Internet: "I am a plain woman of uncertain age, standing six feet in my stockings. . . . I scribble a bit for various sporting journals, and I would rather fish any day than go to heaven."

Wish I could've met Fly Rod. She sounds like a gal who was comfortable in her own skin. Plus, I'm partial to fishing.

A Moose Just Goes for It

As you can imagine, we've got quite a few moose in our neck of the woods. So, someone is always telling a moose tale, which is like a fish story, only bigger.

A while back, I'm working at the A&P when in comes Archie Johnson. Archie's what we affectionately refer to in Mahoosuc Mills as a "mangy old fart." He lives in a run-down trailer on the edge of town, tires piled in the yard, blue tarps strewn all over, broken cars up on cinder blocks. I know, sounds like a cliché, but clichés got to come from somewhere. And Archie's livin' proof.

Archie generally keeps to himself. "Lives off the land" would be a nice way to put it. He comes into town once a week for "supplies." Though Archie's looks and odor can be a little off-putting (Archie would never win a gold star for personal hygiene), he's harmless enough.

So I'm ringing Archie out, and I notice that along with the usual—couple cases of Miller Lite, cans of Vienna sausages, Spam, Marshmallow Fluff, Skippy, Wonder Bread, and a few Snickers bars—he has about a dozen bottles of ketchup.

> *A while back, I'm working at the A&P when in comes Archie Johnson. Archie's what we affectionately refer to in Mahoosuc Mills as a "mangy old fart."*

"How you doing, Archie?" I ask.

"Getting by."

"Glad to hear it."

Archie's not much for small talk; that's usually the extent of our conversation. So, I was kind of surprised when he continued.

"Sawed a moose last night."

"You did? Where'd you see it?"

"Didn't. That's why I hit it."

"Goodness, Archie! You all right?"

"No worse for wear."

"And poor Ethel? She okay?" (Ethel's what Archie calls his '65 Chevy half-ton.)

"Hood's a little stove-in is all. Cosmetic."

"How about the moose?"

"DOA. Poor fella didn't stand a chance."

Just then, I get a whiff of Archie's aroma. "I'll bet he didn't," I says. "What'd you do?"

"I sawed it."

"I thought you said you didn't see it, Archie."

"Didn't. I hit him, got out my saw, and sawed him. Put the pieces in the back of the truck and drove home. Them moose is good eatin'. You fry them up, douse them with ketchup, and it's just like eatin' fill-it minyon."

Honest to God! Who needs Rachel Ray when you got Archie Johnson?

So later that evening, I'm telling this story to Charlie, and we get to talking about moose and how hard they are to see in the dark. Unlike a deer, the whites of a moose's eyes don't give them away, mainly 'cause they don't bother to stop and stare at you. The saying doesn't go, "Like a moose caught in the head-lights," does it? No, when a moose sets his sights on something, he just goes for it.

"Sounds like someone else I know," Charlie quips.

"And who would that be, mister?"

"I'm looking right at her."

"Well," I says, "I bet there's a lot we can learn about life from the moose."

"Sure there is, Ida," Charlie says, humoring me. See, you got to understand, my husband considers himself one of the finest

moose hunters in all of Franklin County. "Why don't you look
into it and maybe write a book or something?"

"Well, maybe I will!" And it just took off from there.

Moose Totem

Now, I knew in my gut that if I was going to research
moose and write an entire book, I was going to need help. So,
I enlisted my niece, Caitlin, as my assistant. She really knows
her way around the computer, like kids do nowadays, and she's
pretty commonsensical, too.

Caitlin, who is in her 30s, is my sister Irene's daughter.
Cute as a button, even with that nose ring. She works down to
Mahoosuc Health Food and does a little feng shui consulting on
the side. Let's just say she's up on all the New Agey stuff.

When Caitlin and me first started working on our moose
research, she says to me, "Aunt Ida, you and your friends chose
to call yourselves the 'Women Who Run with the Moose.' We
need to find out what having the moose as a totem means."

"Totem?" I says. "You mean like a totem pole?"

"Not exactly," she explains. "A totem is an animal that is
your symbol—you know, like your zodiac sign. It comes from
the Native American tradition. Each animal represents different
traits."

"How do you know what animal you are?"

"Well, you either choose an animal, or the animal chooses
you. I think you must have had a calling to pick the moose. Let's
see what a moose totem means."

Then her fingers start flying over the computer keys. In seconds she's got an answer. "Look at this!" she squeals. "It says
here on this animal totem website (yes, there is such a thing),

'Moose teach us to value ourselves and reward ourselves for a job well done'!"

"Caitlin," I says, "The Women Who Run with the Moose is founded on that very principle. We reward ourselves all the time. It usually involves shopping or sugar, or better yet, shopping and sugar!"

Caitlin continues, "The Penobscot Indians believe that moose are whales that came up onto land. And that First Woman admired the moose so much, she chose him over all other living things as her mate."

"Well, I like moose and all, Caitlin, but that seems a little extreme. Was this before or after First Man showed up?"

> *"Caitlin," I says, "The Women Who Run with the Moose is founded on that very principle. We reward ourselves all the time. It usually involves shopping or sugar, or better yet, shopping and sugar!"*

She ignored me and kept on reading.

"The moose is the symbol of feminine energies, creativity, and dynamic forms of illumination."

"That makes perfect sense," I say. "As you know, the Women Who Run with the Moose focus a considerable amount of energy into crafts. And in terms of illumination, the older we get, the brighter the light we need in order to see what we're doing!"

Clearly, we were off and running. When it comes to livin' the good life, it turns out you actually can learn a lot from the moose.

How to Use This Book

In addition to sharing facts and suggestions that I have learned from moose research, my own curiosity and the wisdom gleaned from living in Mahoosuc Mills, I have decided to ask some people to help me with a few points. In each chapter, my niece Caitlin will offer some excercises that are little more New Agey and what I call woo-woo. Some of you just might like it. Also in each chapter, my husband Charlie will offer a man's point of view on a few topics. I figured, can't hurt, right?

I've noticed that a lot of self-help books have "action steps" at the end of each chapter. You know, changes you can make or exercises you can do to overhaul your life. I don't know about you, but I often find them, well, kind of daunting.

Action steps are just too big, in my opinion, so, to get you goin', I'm advocating little things you can try to make your life even better. They are not calls to action. They're more like suggestions. No big deal. Just easy-peasy!

Not all of the steps will work for you. Just cherry-pick the ones that do. 'Cause here's the deal: Livin' the good life means different things to different people. This book is all about livin' your *own* good life, not mine or anybody else's. But having an open mind and being willing to try new things is key.

 Straight Talk from the Barcalounger

Just as she does at home in our double-wide, you'll notice Ida does most of the talking in this book. But from time to time, I'm going to add my two cents, because both Ida and me think it is important to hear a man's point of view.

I've been on many a moose hunt in my day. Moose are magnificent creatures and awesome to behold in the wild. Big, too. Your males are gonna run around a thousand pounds, the female a little less. They eat plants, up to fifty, sixty pounds of 'em a day. And they don't have any upper front teeth.

As a rule, they're peaceful creatures, unless riled. Use your head and you shouldn't have much problem. And if you see a moose with a calf, for God's sake give 'em a wide berth or you'll be sorry.

If you want to hunt moose in Maine you have to enter the moose lottery, which is too complicated to explain here. Only a limited number of licenses are available, and it's as thrilling as winning the Megabucks when your name is picked.

Between me and the boys, Bud, Smitty, Pat, Tommy, and Junior, one of us usually gets a license, so we have an excuse to go "hunting." This usually involves beer, beef jerky, and card playing in the "clubhouse," which is just an old hunting camp up our way. I'd tell you where it is, but then I'd have to kill you.

 Caitlin's New Age Nook: A Little More Woo-Woo
As Aunt Ida mentioned, she has graciously allowed me to contribute little exercises here and there that have come to me through my practices of feng shui, yoga, and meditation. Since she says some of them are a little too "woo-woo" for her, and may be for you, too, we're also going to add Aunt Ida's modification if she thinks we need one.

Earlier in this chapter we discussed totems. What's your animal totem? The first animal that came into your mind when you read that question is a good bet. Or how about an animal that you dream about or the one you always check out first at the zoo? Still unsure? Go online and search "finding your animal totem" to find quizzes and helpful meditations. Once you've found your totem, look up the attributes and see if they resonate for you. Another thing you can do is to buy animal totem cards. Shuffle the deck and pull one at random when you need

15

guidance, or pull one out every morning, like checking your horoscope.

Aunt Ida Tweaks It: A Little Less Woo-Woo

I'm glad the moose chose me, 'cause I don't know if I could've figured that out on my own—although I've always had a fascination with moose.

Now, I know Caitlin's exercise is kind of woo-woo, but, what the heck, give it a go. Figuring out your animal totem can be fun. Do it with a group of friends at a party. Before you know it, you'll be peeing your pants you're laughing so hard.

For example, Shirley thinks she's a butterfly, but she strikes me more like a porcupine, 'cause, between you and me, there are times when Shirley can be kind of prickly.

Two

You Catch More Flies with Honey

I'm going to kick this whole thing off by telling you the most important part of livin' the good life, 'cause, let me just say up front, I've read a few self-help books in my time. What bugs me the most about 'em is that all through the book they keep saying how they're going to tell you the number one thing you can do to achieve whatever it is they're peddling. They build it up, teasing you, trying to get you to read more. Then, when they finally divulge their big revelation at the end of the book, it's kind of anticlimactic. Well, I'm going to cut right to the chase. The most important thing in life is: Have a positive attitude. I think—and many studies back me up—that having a positive attitude not only helps you live longer, but it also makes life a heck of a lot easier and frankly, much more fun.

I know what you're thinking. Looking at the sunny side and always being nice takes a lot of effort. It's exhausting, right? Well, being a grump's not really any easier. It's hard work trying to see the downside of everything. Although, some folks manage to do just that.

I remember back in high school I worked as a chambermaid and waitress at Henderson's Lodge and Cabins up on Moose Megantic Lake. Folks from away would come stay a coupla weeks, a month, some the whole summer. Most people were real nice, but every once in a while, we'd get somebody who was just flat out committed to being miserable. They'd complain, "This egg isn't cooked right!" or "What do you mean you don't have phones in the rooms?" or "The loons are keeping me up at night!" The loons were keeping them up? I mean, come on—you're in Maine!

> They'd complain, "This egg isn't cooked right!" or "The loons are keeping me up at night!" The loons were keeping them up? I mean, come on—you're in Maine!

There's just no pleasing some people is what I thought at first. Then it dawned on me: These folks love being grumpy, so maybe I am pleasing them! In fact, I bet I just made their day.

Independent and Good-Natured

Look, being positive isn't as hard as it may seem. It only gets dicey when we either depend on someone else to make us happy, or try too hard to make another person happy. Here's a clear example of how we need to be more like the moose.

Moose are independent and generally good-natured creatures. As a Mainer, or "Maineiac," as we call ourselves, I come from a long line of independent thinkers. For example, not only is the moose our state animal, but the Maine state flower—get this—isn't even a flower. It's a pinecone!

These traits of being independent and good-natured are tied together in my mind. Being independent means not being dependent, right? To me, that includes not depending on others to make me happy. Not on my friends. Not on Charlie. Not on anyone. I believe we are all responsible for our own good time. I don't know about you, but it makes me feel lighter just thinking about that, because if you are responsible for your own good time, it follows that you're not responsible for anybody else's, right?

Now, I'm not saying you should stop doing nice things for people, or that you should only think about yourself. On the contrary, keep doing what you're doing. Just stop trying to make people happy who don't want to be. I'm emphasizing this 'cause it happens to be a tough lesson for me, one it seems that I have to relearn over and over.

Avoiding the "Yeah, buts"

We have this couple in Mahoosuc Mills, Claudia and Kurt Peavey, or the "Yeah, buts," as Charlie and me call them. Don't matter what you say to 'em, they come back with, "Yeah, but . . ."

I'm sure you know folks like this. You can't win for losing with this pair, even when you pay them a compliment.

"Gee, Claudia," I'll say, "that sure is a pretty scarf you're wearing."

To which she replies, "Yeah, but it's 'dry clean only.' If I'd have known, I wouldn't have bought it."

What do you say to that?

Even when you agree with the Peaveys (and I've tried it), they'll still "yeah, but" you. Happened to Charlie just the other day.

Kurt goes, "I just heard they finally extended Saturday hours down to the transfer station. It's open 'til three now."

"I know." Charlie says. "That'll make it easier for us to get down there."

"Yeah, but I don't know where the town's going to find the money to pay Ernie and them to work those extra hours."

Some people are just born contrary. Caitlin says they are "on their first life." I don't know about that, but I do know that about all you can do with folks like this is let them stew in their own grumpiness.

Happy in Mahoosuc Mills Is . . .

- Folks going into or leaving the Busy Bee Bakery. If that don't make you happy, nothin' will!
- Kids on the horse-drawn sleigh ride out in Bucky DuMont's field. (Part of our Down Home Holiday Festival, which used to be the Down Home Christmas Festival, but we are now politically correct.)
- Anyone not getting pink-slipped down to the mill come payday!
- Our little dog Scamp when I get home from work. Or when we go for a walk. Or when I give him a treat (which Charlie says I do too often. But I say, "Scamp gets bonus points just for being so darned cute!") Actually, Scamp looks happy most of the time. I think that's because whatever he's doin' at the moment is his favorite thing. There's probably a lesson in there, somewhere.

The Ripple Effect of Happiness

Choosing to be upbeat, focusing on the positive, is like tossing a stone in a pond. You start a ripple, one that just keeps widening outward. There is an old saying, "You can catch more flies with honey than you can with vinegar." Well, the Maine state insect ain't a honeybee for nothing.

I see the power of a positive attitude in action every time my sister, Irene, and me go shopping together. I love shopping with my sister. Well, I love shopping period, but it's especially fun with her. First off, it makes both of us feel close to our mother. She was one heck of a shopper, our mother, and the three of us had many a good time pounding the pavement down to the Bangor Mall. Mom's been gone eight years now, but her shopping spirit still burns bright in Irene and me.

One day last winter, I don't know, I just needed to get out of Dodge. Our double-wide can feel mighty close by the middle of February, if you know what I mean. The tip-off? I start feeling like Charlie is taking up more than his fair share of space. That's when I know it's time to pick up the phone and organize some kind of field trip. Irene was feeling kind of antsy, too, so each of us took a mental health day from work and went off to the Bangor Mall.

We stopped by the Busy Bee first on our way out of town, of course, and we each got one of Babe's bacon biscuits with cream cheese filling. Oh, mister man: It's a light fluffy biscuit with crispy bacon pieces baked into the batter with herbed cream cheese oozing from the middle when you take a bite. Two of those babies and a couple of rockets of coffee, and we were in Bangor in no time!

Before getting out of the car, Irene and me have this little tradition. We say a prayer: "Mom, please guide us in our shopping today. May we find what we're looking for, and let it be on sale! Amen." And we're off.

Whenever we go shopping, we always bring along "our colors." That's this little notebook with swatches of fabric in it. See, way back when, just as "Color Me Beautiful" was taking off, Irene and me thought it would be a hoot to take Mom and get our colors done. I think we were celebrating her sixtieth birthday, and we'd heard of this gal in Portland through someone who worked with Irene at the time (can't remember her name, but it don't matter now.)

Anyways, we drove south, got a hotel room, and the next day went to have our colors done. The thing I remember most was the three of us in the car, laughing and joking around.

> *Before getting out of the car, Irene and me have this little tradition. We say a prayer: "Mom, please guide us in our shopping today. May we find what we're looking for, and let it be on sale! Amen."*

The instructions were to arrive wearing no makeup at all and a beige top. 'Course, none of us had a beige top; we're really not beige people, if you know what I'm saying. We wore light-colored tops instead, good enough. But the "no makeup" clause? That was asking a lot.

The three of us hadn't left the house without makeup for years. Decades even! And there we were, driving around the big city of Portland with no makeup on except a little lipstick. I know, technically lipstick is makeup, but come on! We couldn't go completely bare-faced! That's just cruel and unusual punishment.

I says to Irene, who was driving, "Whatever you do, don't get in an accident. We don't want anyone to see us looking like this!"

"No," our mother agrees. "No one except you and your father has seen me without makeup in forty years!"

Irene asks, "What about the doctor when you had your gallbladder out?"

"Are you kidding? They told me not to wear makeup, but I managed to put on lipstick, under-eye concealer, and blush before they wheeled me into the OR. Heck, that doctor was a nice-looking guy!"

Irene and me almost peed our pants, we got to laughing so hard.

Turns out, color-wise, we were all "springs," though apparently I'm an early spring while Irene and Mom are late springs. From then on, the three of us shopped with our colors. Irene and me still do. By now, of course, we don't have to look at our color books as often, but if we're on the fence about something, it's good to have 'em handy.

So last week, our little prayer said, we were in a dressing room at Macy's trying on clothes and giving each other opinions on things like only sisters can. I'm looking at Irene in this dress she's got on that's just not working. "Too Barbara Bush," I says. That got her going.

Meanwhile, I'm modeling this cute lacy top, looking really sharp, and Irene just shakes her head. She goes, "Marsha Twombley," referring to this girl we went to high school with.

"No! That slutty?"

"Ida, what does the sparrow say, huh?"

And together we go, "Cheap, cheap, cheap!" and laugh some more.

Just as we're heading off to get more stuff to try on, this woman stops us.

"What do you think of this dress," she asks. "Is it too dowdy-looking?"

Irene jumps in, "Um, I don't think it's the dress so much as the color."

I agree. "That purple's doing nothing for you. What size is that?"

"Fourteen."

"Okay," Irene says, "let's go look for it in a different color. I'm thinking sky blue."

"Or sea-foam green," I says, and off we go with the gal.

See, that's the magical thing about shopping with Irene. We enjoy each other's company so much, we're having so much fun, people are drawn to us. Suddenly, we become like independent style consultants. Irene and me expect good things to happen, so they do.

> *"I want to look good,"*
> *she says, "but be*
> *comfortable, too."*
>
> *"Honey," I reply, "that's*
> *a tall order. As they*
> *say, 'You got to suffer*
> *to be beautiful.' "*

We end up spending about fifteen minutes with a complete stranger, who looked fabulous in her new blue dress, by the way. Then, Irene and me go to Super Shoes, and each of us get a pair of shoes using their "BOGO" deal (buy one pair, get the second pair half price), splitting the cost. We did a little consulting there, too, for a young lady who was looking for a pair of dress shoes. She kept reaching for these old-lady pumps.

"I want to look good," she says, "but be comfortable, too."

"Honey," I reply, "that's a tall order. As they say, 'You got to suffer to be beautiful.' "

"Look at these!" goes Irene, picking up a pair of black strappy shoes. "Talk about fabulous! I guarantee these'll make your legs look longer."

"Yup," I agree, "and by doing that, it'll take ten pounds off your appearance."

"Really?" goes the girl. This all seemed like news to her. Kids today! Wouldn't you know, a few minutes later, the three of us are in the checkout line together, and she's thanking us for picking out her shoes.

Then Irene and me went for lunch at Friendly's, where we had the cutest little waitress, Bridget. She asked if we had the coupon for the free large sundae. We didn't. Bridget says, voice lowered to a whisper, "I have a couple extras I'll give you."

Wasn't that sweet? The ripples of happiness that we had started earlier in the day had eventually washed right back onto us. So Irene and me both had our favorite: butterscotch sundae with butter-crunch ice cream.

Around two-thirty, we called it quits. We're loading our bargains into the car and Irene goes, "Mom was with us today!"

"That she was."

And looking back at the mall, hands over our hearts, we say, "Thanks, Mom."

 Caitlin's New Age Nook: It's All a Matter of Perspective

I'd like you to try this exercise. Take your hand (it doesn't matter which one), make a fist, then extend your index finger. Now raise this hand over your head, a little in front of you where you can see it. Going clockwise, slowly trace a circle with your hand in the air, like you're drawing a dinner plate with the tip of your finger. Keep circling clockwise as you bend your elbow into a 90-degree angle and move your hand down to chest level. Now look down at your finger. What direction is it going? That's right: counterclockwise. Try it again. Circle your hand clockwise above your head and move it down. What's going on here?

Simple: Your hand keeps circling the same way, but you're looking at it from a different angle. The only thing that's changed is your perspective. Sometimes all it takes to change a negative attitude to a positive one is a different perspective on the situation.

Aunt Ida's Tweak
Can't think of one. Isn't that Caitlin clever, though?

Hard Things Happen

When life throws you a curveball, focusing on the positive isn't always as easy as Caitlin's little exercise. While the first step is deciding to change your perspective, the second is recommitting to that decision every day. And in the end, time works its magic.

When Charlie and me got married, we were looking forward to starting a family. I couldn't wait be a mom, and I knew Charlie would make a wonderful dad. All of our friends were getting pregnant, just like that, and we were not. And, believe you me, it wasn't for lack of trying! More time passed, and I kept going to baby showers for everyone else. The stork just wasn't making an appearance at our double-wide.

> *All of our friends were getting pregnant, just like that, and we were not. And, believe you me, it wasn't for lack of trying!*

Finally, we decided to go see a doctor down to Bangor. I'll spare you the details. Let's just say, it didn't help. Every few months, we'd get our hopes up only to be disappointed again. It just plum wore us down. In the end Charlie and me shook our heads and agreed: It wasn't meant to be.

Then one evening at supper—after I'd been down in the dumps for weeks, which isn't like me—Charlie puts his hand on mine and says, "Ida, I know it's hard, but don't you think it's time we moved on?"

That Charlie!

"You're right, honey. We can't spend the next fifty years looking back at what might have been. Maybe we should make a list of all the things we can do now that we won't be having kids."

I was just sort of joking around, you know? But Charlie smiles at me and goes, "That, sweetheart, seems like a great place to start."

So that's what we did. We made a list. It was kind of liberating, really. It didn't happen overnight, but we stuck with it, and eventually we were able to let go of a whole way of thinking that was dragging us down. We started doing things on our list. We turned the room that was going to be the nursery into my craft workshop, and Charlie bought a table saw for his shed out back. We got our first camper and started traveling.

On our tenth anniversary, we renewed our wedding vows. We had a ceremony, party after, photos, the whole nine yards. I think that's when our marriage really began. The first decade was just practice.

Hard things happen. It's just part of life. It's how you react to those things that can make or break you. Staying positive isn't always easy. But trust me, I know from experience that by changing your perspective and looking for things to appreciate, you'll have more days filled with appreciation.

Go with the Flow

Hands down, I think what gets in my way most often when trying to maintain a positive attitude is my expectations. You know, I'm all jacked up about the Fourth of July picnic, looking forward to it all week, got a new outfit and everything, and, that morning, a monsoon. Or, I can't wait for the new Hugh Jackman movie. Then I go and not only is the plot kind of weak, but its one of those movies where Hugh has unattractive facial hair and bad hygiene. Boy, that kind of thing can cloud over your sunny disposition in a hurry. Alas, big expectations can lead to big disappointments.

Caitlin, who considers herself a Buddhist (it seems harmless enough) says, "Aim for one hundred percent intention, zero attachment."

"Sounds good, Caitlin, but what does that mean?"

"Well," she says, "you set your intention, like 'I'm going to have a good time at that picnic coming up,' or whatever. But you don't project ahead to what that good time is going to look like. You don't try to fill in all the details. If you leave yourself open to whatever happens, you're less likely to be disappointed."

"You mean, go with the flow?" I says.

"Right! It's about being open and curious about what's happening, but not trying to control it."

"Okay, so say we're going to a bean supper down to the Congo Church, and I have my heart set on the peanut butter pie. I mean, I'm thinking about it all week. Come Saturday, we're running late, and by the time we get there, the peanut butter pie is gone. Well, I'm going to be miffed!"

"Sure," Caitlin continues, "but if you think, I'm going to have fun at the bean supper this week, pie or no pie . . ."

28

"Ooh, that's too hard."

"It takes practice. Every time you start thinking about that peanut butter pie, stop, and bring yourself back to your intention: I'm going to have fun at the bean supper, period."

"Then, if there isn't any peanut butter pie, it's no big deal?"

"Right. If you're less attached to that, and open and curious about other options, you may be pleasantly surprised."

"Well," I says, "Estelle Fournier's lemon meringue is pretty tasty, too. It's been a while since I've had a slice of that!"

A Wasted Smile

You've heard the question, "If a tree falls in a forest and no one is around to hear it, does it make a sound?" Maybe, maybe not. I wasn't there, so I don't really care.

But, I was reminded of it last week when Charlie and me were out walking Scamp, and we were passed by a jogger coming the other way. He's this guy from away who moved in down the street. We see him out jogging quite a bit. Meaning, it's not like we're strangers.

So I do what I usually do when we see people on our morning jaunt. I smile and say, "Good morning!" I may even throw in, "Beautiful day, huh?" or "Haven't we had a nice summer?" That kind of thing.

And for whatever reason, this guy never smiles back or says "hi" or acknowledges my greeting in any way. Whatsoever. It's bizarre!

So we keep walking, and I says to Charlie, "Well, that was a wasted smile."

"Ah, you don't know. Maybe he's just having a bad day."

29

"What? Every time we see him? I know he's got those ear thingys in, he's listening to something, doesn't want to be disturbed. But come on! You can give a little wave or something, can't you? Acknowledge your neighbors? Sure you can."

But later, I got to pondering what I said, and I'm like, "Hold on a minute! Can a smile really be wasted, Ida?" Well, I come to the conclusion, no, it can't. 'Cause smiling makes you feel good. I looked it up. It does something to your brain that I don't really get, but scientists say that the shear act of smiling makes you happier, even if you weren't feeling happy to begin with. It don't stop there. These researchers say smiling does just about everything for you that you can think of except make your bed. It helps you feel less stressed, gets you outta your funk, lowers your blood pressure and even boosts your immune system. You can get those same things from exercising, but, seriously?

'Course, I think in order to get the true benefits of smiling, you gotta be all in. You have to turn on your light. Meaning, you need to smile with your whole face, including your eyes. I'm sure you've seen those folks where their mouth is smiling, but their eyes are not. Yes, we've all had bad days, but that's just spooky!

I wonder if there's some people who go through their whole life without turning on that light. You know, like a computer in constant sleep mode, reserving their energy. For what, I ask? Smiling is like plugging in and recharging your mind and body.

Creating More Ripples of Happiness

Okay, here's another exercise for you. Ready? Try smiling at everyone you meet. Sound too woo-woo? What the heck, give it a shot. Once you're comfortable with it, try moving to the intermediate level: Smile and actually say "hi." Or go for broke:

> *When I see someone, young or old, who's made at least some effort to look sharp—I don't care if it's a complete stranger—I'll say, "That sure is a handsome tie you're wearing," or, "Oh, what a cute tattoo! Is that a worm coming out of the apple?"*

Smile, say "hi," and then compliment the person on an article of clothing they're wearing, hold the door open for them or something. That's an advanced maneuver, I know, but how many times have you been somewhere and really loved how sharp someone looked and didn't say anything? That's a missed opportunity for perking people up. Try it tomorrow for an hour, the morning, or maybe the whole day.

I say nice things all the time while standing at my register down to the A&P. It's a kick. When I see someone, young or old, who's made at least some effort to look sharp—I don't care if it's a complete stranger—I'll say, "That sure is a handsome tie you're wearing," or, "Oh, what a cute tattoo! Is that a worm coming out of the apple?"

Oh, occasionally you'll get the grumpster who acts like you're violating their privacy by paying 'em a compliment. Don't take it personal; the poor dears can't help themselves.

But most folks are appreciative. Do it and watch what happens. Suddenly the person stands up a little straighter and smiles, and day-to-day living seems just a little more hopeful.

Straight Talk from the Barcalounger: Don't Take Things so Personal!

Women take things way too personal. They might think, "Marge is mad at me because she didn't call me back." And really, Marge is probably just busy, or home sick with the flu, or plain forgot. Happens! You don't see us guys getting bent out of shape like this.

When was the last time you heard a guy say, "Last Sunday when me and the boys got together, I told that story again about the time when we were out hunting and Junior got blind drunk, went out to take a leak, and got lost on his way back to the cabin. I know I shouldn't have brought that up 'cause I think I embarrassed him, and now Junior's probably mad at me. It's been a week, and he hasn't called!"

No way. Guys just don't operate like that.

Women always seem to be making up stories in their head about why someone is doing what they're doing, or not doing what they think they should be doing. I say, get over it. If you want to be happy, don't take things so personal.

Today's a New Day

Some people truly believe the world is out to get them. I used to feel that way sometimes when I was PMS-ing. (Still do from time to time. Everybody does.) But nowadays, if I start going down that path, I try to stop and remember something Grampy Gilbert used to say when we were fishing.

Grampy was kind of winding down with the guiding by the time I come along. Who could blame him? He still took folks out, just not as many, and only for day trips. Truth be told, I think he'd just as soon gone fishing only with me.

When we had a fishing date planned, I'd lay my clothes out the night before, and my mother'd set my alarm for five. Didn't need it, though. I was up and ready. Never late, Grampy'd drive up in his battered old pickup. I'd grab my gear, my lunch bag, and off we'd go.

Early on, I hadn't developed a feel for fishing yet. I'd see how many fish Grampy'd catch and get discouraged—you know, start thinking the fish were conspiring against me, deliberately choosing Grampy's line over mine.

> I'd see how many fish Grampy'd catch and get discouraged—you know, start thinking the fish were conspiring against me, deliberately choosing Grampy's line over mine.

"I'm never going to catch any fish!" I'd whine the way kids do, you know.

"*Mon p'tit chou*," he'd say. ("My little cabbage." Doesn't sound like a term of endearment, but it is.) "*Mon p'tit chou*, if you think like that, well, that's what you're going to get. Me? I think, today is a new day. I can't wait to see how many fish I'm going to catch!"

How's that for having a positive attitude?

Gettin' Going

* The next time you're thinking, "That person let me down, so my day is ruined," stop and ask yourself, "What can I do right now to take responsibility for my own happiness?"
* Pay attention to how you talk to yourself in your head. Be on the lookout for those pesky "yeah-buts." Think of that "but" as a toilet flush. No matter how wonderful the "yeah" part of the sentence sounds, the "but" cancels it out. It flushes it down the toilet. Once you start paying attention, those "yeah-buts" will begin to disappear from what you're saying and from how you're thinking.
* Could you improve a situation with a change in perspective? What's another way to look at it? Write down a few.

- Practice letting go of expectations and being more open to what's actually happening.
- For an hour, a morning, or a whole day, try smiling at everyone you meet. When you're comfortable, move on to intermediate and advanced levels of this exercise and watch for the ripples!
- The next time you're starting to take something too personal and concocting a story about why someone is doing what they're doing, stop and give yourself a reality check. "Is this really happening, or am I just making this up? Do I have all the facts?"
- Remember Grampy Gilbert's words: "Today is a new day; I can't wait to see how many fish I'm going to catch!" At any time during the day, you can choose to start over, take responsibility for your happiness, change your perspective, and look for things to appreciate.

Three

How Many Points in Cabbage Soup?

It's easier to live the good life if you're healthy and relatively fit. A moose naturally eats right and gets plenty of exercise. I don't know about you, but I don't always do the same. As the years go by, though, I'm more forgiving of myself and am slowly moving beyond the "all or nothing" game plan and figuring out what works for me. I'm with Mark Twain on this one: "All things in moderation, including moderation."

Living the good life is about balance, and this is especially true when it comes to good health. I have two rules when it comes to diet and exercise.

1. Avoid foods that say *fat-free* or *light* that aren't meant to be that way, like fat-free half-and-half and light butter. They are abominations of nature, probably loaded with chemicals, and don't taste that good anyways. My advice? Eat the real stuff, only less of it. My only exception is the chemical "butter" they put on popcorn at the movies. I ask for extra of that, 'cause you gotta walk on the wild side every now and then.

2. Do not attempt any sport with a capital "X" in the name, as in X-treme anything. If you're reading this book, you're too

old for that nonsense to begin with. Besides, you could fall and break a hip.

Be a Twig Eater

When it comes to a healthy diet, we could learn a thing or two from the moose, which eats a combo platter of water plants, leaves, woody plants, and twig tips, complemented with a garnish of bark. (Reminds me of the last diet I tried.) In fact, the name moose comes from the Algonquian Indian word for "twig eater." So, this ain't rocket science. Get in touch with your inner moose by eating your fiber.

We all know that adding fiber to our diet is a good thing. It lowers cholesterol and helps control blood sugar. But, there's a difference between knowing what's good for you and *doing* what's good for you. Heck, I have a busy life, same as you. What with work, shopping, keeping the house tidy, and micromanaging Charlie, it's hard to find time for the things I know I'm supposed to do to stay healthy. It's not like we're all movie stars who have some top chef preparing our meals for us while we work out with our personal trainer. Wouldn't that be nice, huh?

Get It Over With Early in the Day

Listen, I've learned through experience that it takes more energy to avoid doing something than actually doing it. So, what is my approach to good health? Get it over with early in the day.

Here's my routine:

I get up and drink two eight-ounce glasses of water (I try to hold off on the Moxie 'til late morning). Then I take a two-mile walk with my friend, Betty. Walking with a friend helps pass the time. Plus, you burn all those extra calories gabbing, which is a good thing, 'cause to be honest, most of the time our mouths are moving faster than our feet.

Alas, neither the walking nor talking has helped me lose this extra twenty pounds. But the good news is, carrying around an extra twenty pounds qualifies as "weight-bearing exercise," so I figure I've got the osteoporosis thing under control.

> *Carrying around an extra twenty pounds qualifies as "weight-bearing exercise," so I figure I've got the osteoporosis thing under control.*

When I get home from walking, I drink another glass of water and launch into my beauty regime. This involves cleansing, exfoliating, and moisturizing my body with a whole arsenal of products that say things like *age-defying*, *anti-wrinkle*, *alpha hydroxy*, and *Pro-Retinol* on their labels and include enough vitamin A, E, and C to meet the minimum daily requirement—if smearing it all over your body counts.

Once I'm lubed up, made up, and dressed up, it's time for breakfast. By now, of course, I'm starving. I mean, I'm so hungry even my high-fiber cereal looks good. It doesn't taste like much of anything, but it sure looks good. To enhance it, I add a teaspoon of ground-up flaxseed and some blueberries. Years ago, Dr. Oz was on *Oprah* and told her to do that, and for some reason it stuck in my head. Besides, I figure what's good enough for Oprah's good enough for me. The flaxseed adds to the fiber, he says, and has "omega-3 fatty acids," which I'm trusting doesn't add to the overall fat situation. The blueberries ramp it up a notch because they're filled with antioxidants (whatever those are), making them a "superfood." 'Course, if you live in

Maine, you've known forever that blueberries are a superfood, especially them little wild ones.

On top of the fiber, omega-3, and super antioxidants I pour some skim milk, and the chomping begins. It's a good thing Charlie isn't much of a talker in the morning; it would be hard to hear him over my crunching.

I wash everything down with two cups of coffee. Right now they're saying coffee is good for you. (Don't tell me any different if it's changed!) Even better, coffee now counts toward the eight glasses of liquid you're supposed to drink each day. I've finally weaned myself off half-and-half, and now put whole milk in my coffee. (I know I should be trying to work my way down to 1 percent, but that's the best I can do right now. It's a quality-of-life issue.)

Wait, I'm not done! I pour myself yet another glass of water and take my multivitamin and a tablet of L-glutamine. I have no idea why I take L-glutamine. One day I was at the Rite Aid, and there on my list was "L-glutamine." Yes, I thought, that's definitely my handwriting. But I had no recollection whatsoever of writing it, and no idea what the heck it's for. I must have read about L-glutamine somewhere in a magazine and thought it would be good for me, so I bought it. When I got home, I searched through every magazine in the house, but I couldn't find the article that told me why I should buy L-glutamine. I spent ten bucks on it, though, so I take it. I'm hoping it's for memory loss!

> *I searched through every magazine in the house, but I couldn't find the article that told me why I should buy L-glutamine. I spent ten bucks on it, though, so I take it. I'm hoping it's for memory loss!*

By nine a.m., I've exercised, moisturized, eaten my fiber, omega-3, and antioxidants, taken my vitamins and L-glutamine, and drank six of my eight glasses of liquid. Not bad, huh? Then, I pop a baby aspirin and just coast the rest of the day.

Maine Has Plenty of Moxie

As you can imagine, Mahoosuc Mills is not really an action-packed hotbed of activity, so it caused quite a stir a while back when, at the monthly meeting of the Mahoosuc Mills Historical Society, we had ourselves a special guest speaker: Merrill Lewis, president of the New England Moxie Congress. After all, most everyone 'round here drinks Moxie. And it's Maine's official soft drink. No kidding! Back in 2005, the governor signed a bill leaving no doubt about it.

Well, Merrill just dazzled us with his encyclopedic knowledge of all things Moxie. His "Moxie Congress" is really more like a kind of a Moxie fan club, I guess, made up of people who drink Moxie, collect Moxie memorabilia, and get together for parades and such. They wear orange, of course, 'cause that's the color of the Moxie can. I'd have bought a cap or something, you know, as a souvenir, but alas, orange is just not in my color book. Merrill, though, is this nice-looking gentleman of a certain age, with a good head of white hair and a Florida tan, and he looked just famous in it.

He told us how Moxie is the oldest bottled soft drink in the U.S. (1884), and how it's always been associated with Maine because its inventor, Dr. Augustin Thompson,

> They wear orange, of course, 'cause that's the color of the Moxie can. I'd have bought a cap or something, you know, as a souvenir, but alas, orange is just not in my color book.

39

come from over there in Union. "Moxie Nerve Food" he called it originally, and claimed it could do just about everything shy of making your bed. Its "distinctively different taste" was endorsed by none other than Ted Williams and President Calvin Coolidge, and, according to Merrill, Moxie helped win WWII. (Kind of a stretch, I thought, but we all went with it.) He told us how they added a new wing to the Matthews Museum of Maine Heritage just to house a thirty-three-foot-high Moxie bottle once used as a Moxie stand. It was later converted into a house that people actually lived in. Remember, we're talking fanatics here.

We had a little reception after Merrill's presentation, and the refreshments were wonderful: mini cherry cheesecakes (the kind you make with the vanilla wafer on the bottom), whoopie pies, and Doris Bishop's famous cream-cheese-and-pineapple dip. And we drank Moxie, of course. I drink Diet Moxie. (I got to cut down on the calories somewhere.) Merrill told me he prefers the Diet, too, because "it tastes more like the original," which struck me as odd. He didn't look all that old to me.

Well, we've been wanting to do it forever, but I think this is finally the year Charlie and me will take a field trip in July down to the Moxie Festival in Lisbon Falls. Celeste and Bud went last year and had a great time. I guess the parade was a hoot, and Celeste had some Moxie ice cream she claims weren't half bad.

How Many Points in Cabbage Soup?

Even though I know what I'm supposed to eat and how much, every once in awhile I get on a jag where I start eating like I'm going to jail. And you can bet your sweet bippy I'm not pounding down brown rice, tofu and steamed veggies. No, more like a vat of macaroni and cheese, and a Cherry Garcia chaser. This could be because I'm stressed or bored or it's Tuesday. Don't matter. But when I realize my fat jeans have become my new skinny jeans, I know it's time to buckle down. 'Cause, honey, the thought of buying new fat jeans is just more depressing than the thought of starting a new diet.

I confess, me and dieting have had a long and sordid history. I swear, I must have tried 'em all. I bet I've lost and regained an entire person over the years, ten pounds at a time. I've done the Aktins and South Beach, and I once went on that Carbohydrate Addicts Diet and dropped fifteen pounds in a month. Really! But you see, I love sweets. I felt very deprived eating nothing but protein and fat. So after a while, I added the carbs back in, but I didn't reduce my fat intake any, and before I knew it, I'd gained back seventeen pounds. All that effort, and I was two pounds in the hole.

My sister, Irene, and me have done Weight Watchers together, God, I don't know how many times. And it works, in a slow, steady way, but while I'm on it I'm constantly thinking about food, which just wears me down after a while. On the WW, every food has a point-value based on protein, sugar, and fat. So while we're on it, all Irene and me talk about is "How many points in that?" or "I just made a macaroni and cheese that's only three points a serving." (Of course a "serving" is about a quarter-cup and dry as all get out.)

I've also gone on those diets where you eat a lot of just one thing, like grapefruit or rice. Probably the wackiest one was the Cabbage Soup Diet. This was about ten years ago now, but something like that is hard to forget.

The thing that attracted me to the Cabbage Soup Diet was the claim that if I went on it for a week, I'd lose ten pounds, guaranteed. That sounds pretty good, you got to admit, much better than counting calories and breads and fruits and starving yourself for a week just to lose a quarter of a pound. This diet sounded easy. All you gotta do is make this soup out of cabbage, assorted vegetables, and tomato juice. You can eat all you want of that. Plus, on the first day, you get to eat all the fruit you want. On the second day, all the veggies. Easy-peasy, right?

I explained the diet to Charlie. I can't say he was exactly enthused, but he said he'd give it a try. (Both of us had porked out something fierce over the winter.)

We started the diet Sunday noon. We couldn't start first thing 'cause there was a pancake breakfast down to the Church of the Nazarene. We couldn't miss that! So after the eight-thirty Mass down to Saint Hyacinth's, we head over there to bulk up a little for the ordeal ahead—you know, to keep up our strength. Oh, were those blueberry pancakes ever tasty! Just plumb-chucka full of them little Maine blueberries, hand-picked by elderly Nazarene women, and topped off with real maple syrup. There's nothing like it.

Needless to say, the cabbage soup was a little anticlimactic after that. But because of the pancakes, we weren't too hungry, even at supper. We both had ourselves a big bowl of the soup. It wasn't too bad, and it filled us up.

As the evening wore on, though, I start to get a little hungry. Charlie, too. I remember we were sitting in the den, watching the tube, and every commercial that come on, Charlie gets up and goes into the kitchen, opens the fridge, and stares in.

"You can eat all the fruit you want, dear," I remind him.

"Oh, goody," he grumbles. By the time we crawled into bed, Charlie must've eaten a pound of green grapes and half a dozen apples.

Well, I was so hungry, I hardly slept. My rumbling stomach kept waking me up. Charlie's snoring didn't help. Finally, I get up and go to the bathroom—you know, for something to do. I come back into the bedroom, and boy oh boy, did it ever smell bad. In his sleep, Charlie must have been, how should I say it, processing his cabbage soup and fruit. I was afraid to get under the covers and stir things up. But I thought, Ida, just stick it out a few minutes, and you won't notice.

> *So I'm laying there, listening to Charlie's emissions, and I start wondering if it is possible to get asphyxiated in that bedroom.*

So I'm laying there, listening to Charlie's emissions, and I start wondering if it is possible to get asphyxiated in that bedroom. I could just picture the headlines: CABBAGE SOUP DIET CLAIMS LIFE OF MAINE COUPLE IN TRAGIC BEDROOM FINALE, or COUPLE PASSES AWAY PASSING WIND, or TWO OLD FARTS DIE OF AN OLD FART'S FART!

I got myself laughing so hard, I woke up Charlie.

"Jeez," he says, "I'm wicked hungry. Think I'll have me another apple."

He gets up, goes into the kitchen. A few minutes later, Charlie comes back into the bedroom, stops, and goes, "Did something die in here?"

"Charlie," I says, "many cabbages have sacrificed their lives so we can look good this summer. Now crack the window a tad, and come back to bed."

Well, the next morning was some rugged. Neither of us had gotten enough sleep, and Charlie was cranky. He said he woke up and the bedroom was freezing.

"Better cold than asphyxiated," I says to him.

Charlie passed on the cabbage soup for breakfast, grabbed a banana instead.

"Charlie!" I says. "You put that back. No fruit today, dear. You want a carrot?"

He stormed out of the house and jumped into his truck. I had to run out after him with his lunch: a Thermos full of cabbage soup, a salad (dry), a cucumber, and a baggie full of carrot sticks and celery. Charlie just grunted and burned rubber as he spun out of the driveway. I'm thinking, It's gonna be a long week.

Truth be told, I wasn't all that excited at the thought of cabbage soup for breakfast, myself. But I was determined. So, I nuked a bowl of soup and cut up some more carrots and celery. I'm sitting there, seven-thirty in the morning, gagging down a delicious bowl of cabbage soup and looking forward to unlimited vegetables for the rest of the day (my heart be still). There's a celebrity on one of them morning shows whining about her love life, and I'm thinking, What the heck are you complaining about?

Well, by eight-thirty I was starving. And I just couldn't get comfortable. The gas pains were darn near crippling! Finally, I decide to walk downtown to Hair Affair for my weekly appointment with Patsy. (She'd been out of town the weekend, and I had to switch my normal appointment from Saturday to Monday.) Ida, I says to myself, you'll feel better once you get your hair done. It's overdue.

So I'm walking downtown, and I swear, every step I take, I let one loose. For two miles! The birds stopped singing, flowers wilted in my wake, squirrels fell from trees. I didn't know how I was going to sit in the chair without Patsy keeling over, but I needed my hair done. Ida, I remind myself, you have to suffer to be beautiful. Just tighten up them vise grips and hold it in.

44

I'm sitting at Hair Affair, my butt cheeks squeezed together so tight I feel like Jane Fonda. Finally Patsy says, "Ida, you seem a little tense today, dear."

Well, that killed the morning. Soon it was time for lunch— oh, goody! See, I eat before I go in to work. I'm just there six hours and only get a coffee break.

The afternoon crawled by. I was absolutely starving. Found myself getting a little snappy with people who were buying things I liked to eat. Five o'clock arrived just in the nick of time.

Charlie comes home from the mill a little after six. His day hadn't been any better than mine. It was Harvey's birthday, so everyone at work chipped in for a cake and ice cream. I give Charlie credit, though. He didn't eat any. He trudges into the den and turns on the tube. I think that's the first time in over forty years of marriage Charlie hasn't asked me what's for supper.

After about fifteen minutes, Charlie comes into the kitchen, looks at me, and says, "You want to go to Bonanza?"

"Give me five minutes to put on some lipstick and get my jacket," I says to him.

Boy oh boy, did we ever pig out! It was like we hadn't eaten in a week. We had Bonanza Burgers, steak fries, and onion rings. Then we stopped by the DQ and got Peanut Buster Parfaits. My God, was it ever good.

When we get home, Charlie goes into the den. I beeline it to the fridge, get out that cabbage soup, and pour it down the garbage disposal. I swear, that soup was so bad even the "pig" didn't want it! Then I grab a Bud for Charlie and a Moxie for me, and we settle down for an evening in front of the tube.

I says to Charlie, "I fed that soup to the pig."

"Good riddance!" he replies.

A little while later, Charlie starts to laugh.

"What's so funny?" I ask.

"You hear that?"

"What?"

"The garbage disposal just farted."

Straight Talk from the Barcalounger: Charlie Weighs In

I can always tell when Ida's dieting. How? Well, between you and me, she's cranky as all get out. The portions get a little smaller at supper, and all of a sudden, I'm not tasting any butter. But the dead giveaway comes later.

See, I like to have a little snack while I'm watching the tube. You know, chips, crackers, nuts, whatever. And okay, maybe I make a little noise eating that stuff.

"Quit that crunching!" she snaps. She could be in another room, it don't matter. She hears it.

The other clue's at breakfast. You know, I usually eat whatever Ida puts in front of me; I'm not fussy. But oatmeal? I'm sorry, that just don't cut it. Sure, I'll thank her, and kind of move it around in the bowl. But on my way to work, I'll stop by the Busy Bee and get their special breakfast sandwich, the "Big Boy," which me and the guys call "The Other Woman," 'cause you got to sneak around to have it, and you feel a little guilty after.

The "No Diet" Diet

Right now I'm in what I call a "no diet" phase. The main thing is, I'm trying to pay attention to what I eat and to slow down when eating it. See, I love food, but I realize that a lot of the time, I'm not really tasting it beyond the first bite or two. Sad to say, my tendency's to pretty much shovel it in. Moose don't do that. They graze. I've never seen a fat moose, so there's definitely something to be learned here.

I'm also trying to stop eating before I'm full. You hear the experts talk about that all the time. "Eat until you're 80 percent full." But how do you measure that?

Lately, I've been remembering Grampy Gilbert joining us for dinner.

"Dad," my mother'd say, "you've still got more food on that plate. Are you all done?"

Grampy would slap his belly and reply, "*Ça suffit.*" (I'm satisfied.) He knew when he was done. Soon as he was satisfied, he'd stop eating. And that, plus all that walking in the woods, accounts for what fine shape he was in. No blubber on that fella. So, I'm trying to eat more like Grampy Gilbert.

'Cause here's the catch, and why the "no diet" is not as easy as it sounds. If you give up dieting, you also have to give up pigging out. Now that's tough! I like pigging out from time to time. Well, I don't like feeling so full I'm going to burst, or waking up in the middle of the night with heartburn. Who does? But it's comforting to know that if things get a little stressful at the A&P, I can have a King Size Snickers bar and feel better. Or if we've just finished supper, and Charlie says, "Ida, how about we go down to the DQ and get a little treat?" I can go. What am I going to do? Be a stick-in-the-mud and say no?

In short, I've found I'm really good at "no dieting," so-so at not pigging out. But I'm working on it.

> *Nowadays you see pictures of yourself from back then and you think, "I weighed a hundred and ten in that picture" ('cause if you're anything like me, you know approximately how much you weighed in every picture ever taken of you).*

It's nice to not be on some kooky diet, starving all the time, and it frees me up from obsessing over when I'm going to eat my three-point snack.

Remember when you were in high school and thought you looked fat? Nowadays you see pictures of yourself from back then and you think, "I weighed a hundred and ten in that picture" ('cause if you're anything like me, you know approximately how much you weighed in every picture ever taken of you). My God! I look so young and thin! (Again, what a difference a change of perspective makes.)

When all else fails and I'm feeling down about my weight (yes, it still happens), I try to remember that. I think, "When I'm eighty years old and see pictures of myself right now, I'm going to be amazed at how young and thin I look."

Now if someone could come up with the no-exercise plan, I'll be all set.

Path of Least Resistance

As I said earlier, I try to walk a couple of miles in the morning with my friend, Betty. We aim for three days a week, but once winter sets in, those good intentions have a way of flying south with the snowbirds. So, I join the gym or sign up for an exercise class down to the Community Center or something. But here's the deal: Sometimes the most exercise I get is writing the check for the monthly fee. It'd be just great if belonging to the gym was enough, but no, you have to actually go. Where's the justice.

Besides, exercising can be dangerous. Did your mom ever scare the you-know-what out of you by saying if you mess with this or that, you'd "poke your eye out"? Well, she wasn't just saying that to scare you. Stuff happens!

On Saturday, I'm being a good doobee, doing some strength training, which is just one of the many things you're supposed to add into your schedule after, quote "a certain age." I have a strength training CD that stars Wendy, a tiny, elf-like woman who looks harmless enough, but let me tell you, she has a sadistic streak. Her weapon of torture is the resistance band. Despite that, I do the CD 'cause it has these ten-minute workouts that target different areas—upper body, lower body, and core. I can wrap my head around ten minutes most days. I figure doing ten minutes consistently is better than thinking about, but not doing thirty minutes, three times a week. Besides, I have to walk Scamp, too, and I'm on my feet all day down to the A&P. So, it's not like I'm some Maine couch potato.

Saturday was a lower body day. I'd already done the running man, a few modified lunges, some plies, and I'm in the middle of doing squat abductions (I know, pretty impressive, huh?). So, I'm busy squatting and abducting, working up a dew, when snap! My resistance band breaks in two. Needless to say, I was a little startled. Scamp, too, though not so much from the snapping as the expletive that may have escaped my lips at that moment. Good thing it wasn't my upper body day, 'cause I might have proved my mother right, and if not exactly poked my eye out, then at the very least gotten slapped in the face by one of them loose band ends. I'm a lucky gal.

I rather suspect the band didn't break because of my massive muscles. Sadly, I think the darn thing was just plumb worn out. Boy, I know how that feels!

So, I'm off to the Wallymart to get me a new resistance band. I figure one every three years isn't too bad. This time, I think I'll use a sharpie and mark the date I bought it on the CD. That way, I'll know when to don my protective eyewear.

Gettin' In Shape For Shopping

Let's face it—when it comes to exercise, it helps to have-someone or something that motivates you. For example, come late October or early November, the Women Who Run with the Moose go into high training. We meet every Saturday and take a power walk, gradually working our way up from two miles to three, then four, topping out at five miles. And, of course, by doing it as a group, you push harder.

Which isn't to say we neglect our upper-body strength. No way! Dot came up with the brilliant idea of walking with our pocketbooks—full, of course, with a couple of hand weights tucked inside. Funny-looking? You bet. We get plenty of honks when the guys drive by, but it's all part of getting in shape for one of our favorite days of the year—Black Friday!

Listen, the Bangor Mall is pretty big. You're starting real early the day after Thanksgiving, and you must be able to go the distance and not get all tuckered out around midday.

You'll be glad you did all that weight-training, too. Those shopping bags get heavy, and it's just not practical to keep running back and forth to the car.

Winning the Super Bowl of Shopping takes planning, so we also have a strategy session to compare lists and create a game plan: who is going where with whom, and, equally important, where we're eating lunch and having snacks.

Taking a time-out every now and then is critical, not just for energy, but for keeping up your morale. Like in any sport, there are fumbles, missed opportunities, and disappointments, so you have to build in time to huddle and bolster each other up.

And sometimes, you have to punt. You know, improvise. The most important thing (and the hardest, really) is being able to assess the situation and adapt your original plan. Or in some cases, throw it out altogether. You may think you're going to buy your sister some nice Isotoner gloves, but then you discover a cashmere scarf they're practically giving away, and it's smack dab in the middle of her color book. You need to be able to seize the opportunity, without hesitation, because in shopping, as in life, if you snooze, you lose!

Exercise in Mahoosuc Mills Is . . .

- Bicep curls down to the Brew Ha-Ha. (Alternate hands when lifting that pint of Bud, and try not to spill.)
- Dancing to Bucky Dumont's band once a month at the Knights of Columbus. (My advice is to come early. By the second set, they start to fall apart.)
- Getting your Ski-Doo onto the trailer. (You might want to rope a young fella in to givin' you a hand. If not, make sure your cell phone's handy and 9-1-1's on the speed dial.)
- Shoveling snow. (Use a scoop as much as you can, and quit before your back does.)
- Chopping wood for the stove. (Heats you up twice!)
- Swatting blackflies. Again, alternate hands.

Are You Choking?

At this point in my life, even a little exercise is better than none at all. It's all about staying ahead of the game health-wise. Visit the dentist. Go for a physical. Get your mammogram. Have a colonoscopy. None of these are my idea of a good time either, but better than taking a second mortage on your dou-ble-wide to finance that surprise vacation down to Maine Med.

Training for Black Friday is all well and good, but a while back, Celeste, Rita, Betty, Dot, Shirley, and me decided we

> *We need to know what to do if we're on one of our field trips, and God forbid, one of us needs first aid or something. Right now, all we have in our first-aid kit is premoistened towelettes, ibuprofen, and Hershey's Kisses.*

needed a cause to get behind—something we could really sink our teeth into besides chocolate. After mulling it over, we thought, Well, we're all women, and we all have hearts, right? Let's make our cause "women's heart health."

Turns out, heart disease is the leading killer of women in the U.S. I lost one grandmother and an aunt to heart attacks, and Betty lost her mother. Meanwhile, Dot's battling high cholesterol, and Rita high blood pressure. Not to mention the fact that I'm an apple shape (or the "French barrel," we call it in our family), which puts me at a higher risk for heart disease 'cause I carry my extra twenty pounds in my middle.

Heart health is also a good choice because the disease is actually something you can work on preventing, as opposed to one of them luck-of-the-draw kind of things like cancer or MS. Plus, they have that whole "Go Red For Women" campaign with the red-dress pins and lots of other nifty red paraphernalia you can buy.

So, we're not only trying to exercise more, we decided to learn CPR, just in case. After all, the Husbands of the Women Who Run with the Moose are all Mahoosuc Mills volunteer firemen and they had to learn CPR. I says to the girls, "If something happened to one of us, our husbands would be able to save our lives, but we couldn't do the same for them. That's just not right. Plus, we're not getting any younger. We need to know what to do if we're on one of our field trips, and God forbid, one of us needs first aid or something. Right now, all we have in our first-aid kit is premoistened towelettes, ibuprofen, and Hershey's Kisses."

It took a while for the girls to get on board with my idea, but eventually they all came 'round. The fact that the CPR class was being given by the Red Cross office in Bangor was an extra incentive: We could make a day of it. You know, have lunch, do a little shopping.

Now, if you're expecting this to be some big story about how all six of us girls got silly with our CPR dummies, practicing mouth-to-mouth and whatnot, I have to disappoint you. And frankly, I was disappointed, too. I thought the class was going to be a lot more fun than it was.

First, they gave us an overview of basic first aid. The key to that is, don't panic, delegate, and make sure someone calls 9-1-1. Easy-peasy. Then, we learned about what to do if someone is choking. But they don't call it the Heimlich maneuver anymore. "Which is a good thing," mutters Shirley, " 'cause that always sounded kind of dirty to me."

If someone is choking, it's basically "5 and 5"—five firm pats on the back and then five of them Heimlich-y moves, repeated until the "foreign substance is dislodged." This is after you go up to the person and ask them, "Are you choking?" Once they reply "yes" by shaking their head (or as Dottie did, by holding up a little piece of paper that read, "No shit, Sherlock!"), then you say, "I know what to do. Is it all right if I help you?" We play-acted all of this stuff like we were auditioning for *Grey's Anatomy* or something.

Then we moved on to CPR, the whole reason we were there. We were each given a dummy to practice on, but really, it was only half a dummy. Which was kind of disconcerting because it looked like we were trying to resuscitate someone who'd been sawed in half by David Copperfield (the magician, not the one in that really long book I never got around to reading). Then we were each given latex gloves and a mouth guard, this paper-towel type thingy with a slit at the mouth so you don't catch something, I suppose.

Once we were all suited up in our biohazard gear, we set to work doing the "breath of life" twice, then thirty compressions, then repeat, repeat, repeat. Let me tell you, after a few minutes of that, we were all getting a little dewy. Celeste says, "This counts as my upper-body workout for the week!" Then we took a multiple-choice test, which all of us passed with flying colors. We got little Red Cross cards saying we were certified to do CPR for a year. That's right; after all that work, it's only good for a year!

The instructor asked us if we wanted to buy a key chain with one of them mouth guards in a plastic pouch attached to it. She also suggested we carry latex gloves in our car.

Us girls decided we didn't really need the gloves or the mouth guard because frankly, we'd only be comfortable doing CPR on someone we know. "Preferably, someone we like," Shirley adds.

"Okay, then," I says. "With a stranger, our game plan is to remain calm and delegate. Meaning, we tell someone to call 9-1-1 and ask if anyone on the scene knows CPR."

"Unless, of course he's cute," Celeste adds.

We agreed hands down: "Unless he's cute!"

 Caitlin's New Age Nook: Breathe!
One of the best things we can do to enhance our overall health is to breathe. Sure, we do it all the time, but most of us are not really taking full, deep breaths. It's something we have to practice. It's easy and only takes five minutes.

Sit on the floor or in a chair in a quiet, calm place. Close your eyes and take a moment to get centered. Feel your butt on the seat and try to be present, in the moment. Then, breathing through your nose, take a deep breath in, counting 1, 2, 3, 4, wait a beat, and exhale: 1, 2, 3, 4. Wait a beat, and repeat. Continue breathing like this, making sure you're really expanding your lungs when you inhale. When exhaling, try to expel all the air from your lungs. Sometimes it helps to quiet your mind by concentrating on feeling the coolness of the air as you take it in, the warmth as you exhale. Do this for five minutes a day, and I think you'll feel an improvement in your overall health.

 Aunt Ida Tweaks It
Breathing's all well and good, but a lot of us don't have five minutes or that calm, quiet place Caitlin mentioned. I say, work it in where you can. Driving in the car is a great place to do deep breathing (skip the "close your eyes" bit though, okay?). Or try it when you're fixing supper or sitting in a paper johnny in the examining room waiting for your gynecologist. Any time you're waiting, really, is a good time to practice taking slow, deep breaths. It calms you down, and makes you feel like you're making the most of your time. So when you find yourself thinking, I'm tired of waiting, use it as an opportunity to practice your deep breathing.

Sleeping Beauty

Now I can't close a chapter on health without addressing a subject near and dear to my heart: sleep. From what I gather, as a country, we're just not getting enough of it, and frankly, it makes me nervous. I don't care who you are—the president, doctors, truck drivers, bankers, a mom in her minivan—how can you do your best if you're sleep-deprived?

In fact, we're so out of whack in the sleep department that people actually brag about it, like it's a good thing. "I need six hours of sleep a night, tops." Or, "Only got four and a half hours of sleep last night, worked all day, and I did a pretty good job." You better hope the person saying that isn't the dentist doing your root canal, right?

Personally, I like getting eight hours of sleep a night. Seven's okay. Anything less than that, and I'm cranky as all get out, slogging around in a fog. The whole day feels unreal.

Now sure, most of us know that not getting enough sleep affects our decision-making abilities and our mood, but studies are now showing it has a big effect on our health, too. When we're sleep-deprived, our body gets all screwed up. We gain weight, our heart health is affected, and so's our immune system. I can't stress this enough: Being sleep-deprived is not a badge of honor, it's a health hazard.

No crazy diets or wacky workouts; the road to good health begins and ends in bed. Now that's doable!

Start from Where You Are

I've found that with health, diet, and exercise, as with most things, it's best to start from where you are. Have you ever said to yourself, "Once I lose ten pounds, I'll . . . " or "I'm going to start using the treadmill as soon as I clean the grout in the bathroom, file these recipes in alphabetical order, and become the ambassador to Tasmania."

My point is: If you're waiting for your life to be perfect before you start living it, your life will consist of lots of waiting and not much living.

Gettin' Going

- Pick one healthy thing you know you should be doing, and get it over with early in the day.
- During one meal, pay attention. Really taste your food.
- Sneak in exercise where you can so it's not so overwhelming. You know the drill: Take the stairs instead of the elevator, park at the far end of the parking lot, etc.
- Ladies, you have a freeweight with you all the time; it's called your pocketbook! Use it for bicep curls, shoulder shrugs, tricep kickbacks. Get creative!
- Practice standing up straight. You'll not only look taller, you'll look thinner, too!
- Balance is really important as we get older. Try standing on one leg with your eyes closed. Do one side, then the other. If you practice this every day, you'll get better at it. Trust me.
- The health decisions you make in your 40s, 50s, and 60s directly effect your quality of life in your 70s, 80s, and 90s. How long has it been since you've been to the doctor or dentist? Are you due for a mammogram, colonoscopy, or stress test? You owe it to yourself to take care of business. Make that phone call. You're worth it.

Four

What Did I Do Wrong to Deserve This Turkey Gobbler Neck?

One day you wake up and you realize your doctors, movie stars, and the president of the United States are younger than you. You find yourself fantasizing about comfortable shoes and bald men with gray hair and a twinkle in their eye. You catch a glimpse of yourself in a store window, and think, "That's a nice looking older woman." You may not feel your age, but every once and awhile your body will remind you.

Doesn't it seem like just as you're hitting your stride in life—family doing okay, work's going good, a little extra money in the bank—your body starts falling apart? What the heck? Your knee goes out and you end up in physical therapy. You strain your back reaching into the car to get that last bag of groceries. Your internal temperature gauge gives up the ghost. It seems like this happens overnight, but if you stop and think about it, you realize that's not really true. Our bodies have been trying to get our attention, but we haven't been taking the hints.

It starts off subtle: slight heartburn after a spicy meal, pop a couple of Rolaids and you're good to go. Maybe you ate a little

too much chocolate and get kind of cranky. That's when you realize, woah! You've just entered an alternate universe.

In this brave, new world, you can be chewing a Junior Mint,
and suddenly realize it has a crunch to it. New formula? No,
that's just the filling from one of your molars that's decided to
give up the ghost. And at this point, they don't fill 'em anymore. No, dear, we're talking a brandy new crown. And guess
what? You've just bought your dentist, his wife and kids a long
weekend in a four-star hotel.

You get a little carried away with Cherry Garcia, Chubby
Hubby, and Everything But the Kitchen Sink. So what? Here's
what—you wake up the next morning with a hangover. Seriously,
a hangover from eating too much sugar! No alcohol involved.
What is this evil planet?

On the death star, you can eat something (who knows what)
and your stomach pumps up to the size of an overinflated beach
ball. Huh? As if that weren't humiliating enough, geysers of fire
erupt like a volcano, sending molten lava up to squeeze your heart
in a vice grip. Rolaids bounce off this beast like marshmallows,
while you, curled in the fetal position on the bathroom floor, welcome the coolness of the tile and pray for relief. Countless "Our
Father's," "Hail Mary's," and a few spontaneous "Jesum Crows"
thrown in for good measure, and poof! The pressure valve magi-
cally releases, sending toxic vapors into the night. Get thee behind
me, Satan! You crawl back to the bedroom, where your sputterin'
husband is blissfully unaware that anything's amiss. Exhausted,
you let slumber take you.

Hey, aging ain't for the faint of heart, but it's better than the
alternative. You just gotta wrap your head around it. There's
something to be said for aging gracefully.....

There's something to be said for aging gracefully, but you don't hear much about that nowadays.

It's more trendy to fight aging tooth and nail. But I say, let's bring the "aging gracefully" concept back.

A moose is a majestic creature, comfortable in its own skin, dealing with life as it comes. Now that's something worth aiming for.

To me, aging gracefully doesn't mean surrendering completely. Au, contraire! It means accepting where you're at, and then doing the best you can with what you've got.

The Powdered Donut Approach

Menopause? I'm pleased to report that me and my friends Celeste, Rita, Betty, and Dot have pretty much cooled off at this point. We've ridden that roller coaster and have gotten off the ride, or at the very least, figured out a way to smooth the track.

Everyone, that is, except Shirley.

Shirley is a slow starter as a rule, and menopause is no exception. She is the skeptic of our group, always hanging back a little, checking things out before resigning herself to whatever new experience we've cooked up. However, once she's committed, she's in full-boat, and I admire her tenacity. Shirley's still hanging in there with our Zumba lessons, even though, poor thing, she just doesn't have a feel for it.

Shirley is six foot tall in her stocking feet, and has this really low voice. Picture Bea Arthur from *The Golden Girls* and that's Shirley. She's our designated driver. Why? She drives a Bonneville. It's the only car that's big enough to hold all six of us. Shirley's driven a Bonneville since I can remember. She special-orders the color, aquamarine, because she thinks it matches her eyes. I can't see it myself, but we humor her.

61

> *Shirley's driven a Bonneville since I can remember. She special-orders the color, aquamarine, because she thinks it matches her eyes. I can't see it myself, but we humor her.*

But, back to the menopause. It's the kind of thing that's different for everyone. It was a nonissue for Celeste, who had a hysterectomy in her thirties. Dotty, who's easygoing to begin with, kind of breezed through, no symptoms at all. Betty was on that horse-pee stuff for a while, then went cold turkey when there was all that hoopla about it. That was rugged, but she toughed it out and made it through. (I think her husband, Pat, is still recovering, though, poor fella.)

For some reason, Rita went the natural route. This came to our attention when all of a sudden she started gaining weight. (Rita's just this little wisp of a thing, so it didn't take us too long to notice.) Finally she goes, "I'm getting really discouraged. I read in *Woman's Day* that wild yams are helpful for the menopause, so I decided to try it. But I've gained ten pounds so far!"

"Jeez," I ask, "are you sure you're doing it right?"

"Well," she says, "I don't know. I've been making that sweet potato casserole, the one with the miniature marshmallows? I bake it on Sundays and eat a little every day."

We love Rita to death, but as Shirley says, "She's not the sharpest knife in the drawer."

Me? Well, I could tell things were changing 'cause my PMS cranked up a notch. I didn't notice it myself, but Charlie sure did. I was waking up in the night sweating, and during the day I could feel myself getting a little fuzzy—you know, trouble remembering things. Not good. I began misplacing stuff, which isn't like me. Then, I lost my car keys.

Well, I didn't know I'd lost them until Charlie comes home from work and says, "Ida, what's this bag of lettuce doing here?"

"What?"

"There's a bag of lettuce hanging on the key rack."

I come into the kitchen, and he was right. I take the lettuce, open the fridge, and go to put it in the crisper. And there are my car keys, sitting in the drawer between a green pepper and the celery. I didn't tell Charlie.

So, I hightailed it to Dr. Lynda, my gynecologist, and asked for drugs. I just don't believe in suffering if you don't have to, and menopause was definitely affecting my quality of life. I'm not on the horse pee, though.

"Ida," Dr. Lynda says, "you've got to do what's right for you." She's got me on that bioidentical stuff, just a low dose. And I feel great!

Then I saw that famous Maine doctor, Christiane Northrup, on public TV talking about menopause, and she agreed with my doc: Just a "light dusting" of hormones can make all the difference. *Light dusting* makes me think of confectionary sugar on a donut. That's how I came to call my menopause treatment the "powdered donut approach."

But poor Shirley's been hit late and hit hard with the menopause, and she's the kind of person who won't even take aspirin for a headache.

> *So, I hightailed it to Dr. Lynda, my gynecologist, and asked for drugs. I just don't believe in suffering if you don't have to, and menopause was definitely affecting my quality of life.*

As a rule, we get together once a month at Shirley's for movie night. That's because she and Junior got one of those big, flat-screen TVs in their family room. But last January when all us girls arrived, we found Shirley propped in front of her freezer, fanning herself with the door.

"To heck with the movie," Dottie says. "This calls for heavy artillery."

"I'm thinking make-your-own ice-cream sundaes," Celeste chimes in.

"Deal!" says Betty. "Rita and me will go get supplies."

While we're waiting, Celeste, Dottie, and me make fans by accordion-pleating paper, and every time Shirley heats up, we fan her down.

"Don't think of it as a hot flash, Shirley," says Dottie. "Think of it as a power surge."

"Dottie," replies Shirley, "if we could harness this energy, I do believe I could power an entire Third World country."

"At least Rhode Island," I says.

Finally, the girls return with the big guns, and the whole thing turns into an ice-cream free-for-all, punctuated now and then by the five of us fanning Shirley down and singing her the chorus of that old Donna Summer song, *Looking for some hot stuff, baby, this evenin'. I need some hot stuff, baby, tonight . . .*

Yikes! It's Turkey Gobbler Neck

I clearly remember the moment I realized things had gotten away from me. One day, I put on my slacks per usual. I turn to check out my backside, and it wasn't there. What happened to my butt, I'm thinking. Just then I catch a glimpse of my profile in the mirror and there it was. Somehow, the fat from my butt had wandered 'round to my stomach. I kid you not.

Once you become aware of this phenomenon, it starts to explain a lot. Like the bulge on my inner thighs. Clearly, that's the bounce that used to be in my breasts. That extra fullness that kept 'em perky has migrated south for the duration, and taken my cleavage with it.

> Who was it that said, "At fifty you get the face that you deserve"? I think I've earned those lines on my face, but, honey, what did I do to deserve this turkey gobbler neck?

Or, I'll be setting the table for supper when I notice that while I wasn't looking, somehow my hands had morphed into my mother's. Then, I start looking at my arms. There's this crepey-ness on the inside of my elbow. So, I go into the bathroom and check the outside of my elbow in the mirror. That's still okay. Not too saggy. But while I'm in there, I take a gander at my face.

I don't mind the lines around my eyes all that much, or the laugh lines around my mouth. I've earned those. They kind of tell the history of my life. Who was it that said, "At fifty you get the face that you deserve"? I think I've earned those lines on my face, but, honey, what did I do to deserve this turkey gobbler neck?

The moose has a flap of skin under its chin called the "bell," which kind of sways when it walks. That didn't use to apply to me, but the older I get, ding-dong. Well, what can you do? It doesn't seem to bother the moose. 'Course, a moose doesn't have to look at themselves in a mirror.

So I'm in the bathroom, checking myself out. I spend a few minutes pulling the skin on my neck taut, which makes me look ten years younger and ten pounds thinner. Then, I hear the potatoes boiling over, and that brings me back to reality.

Oompa Loompa in Aisle 9

I read somewhere that most of the damage we see on our skin today was done before we turned twelve. That's kind of discouraging, 'cause growing up, we'd never heard of sunscreen. Our summertime goal was to get as dark as possible. The girls and me would take a bottle of baby oil, put a few drops of iodine in it, grease up, and sizzle in the sun all day. We thought we were so sophisticated, drinking Shirley Temples from highball glasses and smoking candy cigarettes. I never burned too much because I got that olive tone, Franco-American skin. But poor Rita. Every summer, she looked like a boiled lobster. "Little Red Rita," we used to call her.

If the damage was done way back when, then why am I spending all this money on retinol, alpha hydroxy, and multivitamin lotions? Isn't that kind of like closing the barn door after the horse is out? Well, I'm an optimistic person by nature, so I'm hoping to catch that horse and put it back in the barn before it gets too far gone, if you catch my drift.

My grandmother, oh, she had beautiful skin, milky white and smooth as a baby's bottom, right into her sixties. Back when she was growing up, they always wore a hat or a bonnet to protect their skin from the sun. You've seen them old pictures. It certainly worked for my grandmother. But I don't look good in a hat, and my hair doesn't look good after I take a hat off.

So, if I'm spending time out in the sun, I put on "shade in a bottle," as my sister Irene calls it: sunscreen with SPF 100. I know you're supposed to do this all the time, but who does? Luckily my foundation has SPF 15 (in case I forgot), which is a good thing, because you have to be careful or the left side of your face will age faster than your right side. No, I'm serious! I read this in a magazine somewhere. See, that's the side that gets the most sun when you're driving in your car. You don't want your left side looking like Clint Eastwood, do you? Then wear sunscreen.

If you miss the way you look with a tan but don't want to damage your skin, one option is to use a self-tanner. But I'm not too keen on those. Working at the A&P, let me tell you, I've seen some real disasters. Once in *People* magazine, they were giving out awards to celebrities whose spray tans had gone horribly wrong. They called it the Oompa Loompas, named after those characters in *Willy Wonka*, the ones with the bright orange skin. If you're shopping at the A&P in Mahoosuc Mills and you hear on the loudspeaker, "OLA in aisle nine, OLA aisle nine," you know there is an Oompa-Loompa Alert in aisle nine. Then we take bets on who's going to cash the poor dear out.

> *If you're shopping at the A&P in Mahoosuc Mills and you hear on the loudspeaker, "OLA in aisle nine, OLA aisle nine," you know there is an Oompa-Loompa Alert in aisle nine. Then we take bets on who's going to cash the poor dear out.*

Caitlin's New Age Nook: Reclaiming Your Youth

Getting older doesn't mean your younger selves are gone forever. Those younger versions of you are always there. Here's an exercise to reconnect and reclaim them.

Sit in a quiet, comfortable place. Close your eyes and connect with your breath. Focus on breathing fully and deeply until you're relaxed. Starting at the crown of your head and working down to the soles of your feet, you may want to take the time to consciously relax every part of your body.

Once you are in a state of relaxation, visualize a children's playground. It is a fun, safe place. See yourself as a small child playing in that playground. Watch yourself as you run and play. Once this image is clear, invite your young-girl self to join your child self in the playground. Watch them play together. What are they doing? Swinging, sliding, singing? Add in your teenage self. Maybe they jump rope or play follow the leader. Slowly add yourself into the picture at different ages, right up to the present day. Acknowledge the beauty and strength of these girls, young women, women who were you and still are you. See them standing in a circle, holding hands, and twirling around in one direction and then another, laughing.

When you feel satisfied that you have played enough, picture everyone lining up in order of age, the youngest first. See you, at the age you are now, facing the line. Look at all your vibrant selves, appreciate them, surround them with love and compassion, know they have always done the best they could with what they had. Feel your heart open to them.

When you are ready, hug each of them and invite them into your heart for safekeeping. Do this all the way down the line. When there are no more of you, put your hand on your heart and take a moment to feel their depth of experience, the joy, and the love. Know that all your selves are part of you and always will be. Feel gratitude for them, for you.

When you are ready, return to your breath and slowly become aware of your surroundings. Open your eyes.

Aunt Ida Tweaks It

Okay, I know this one's really, really out there, but try it. I did, and was surprised by how moving it was. Sure, after a while, I could only tell how old I was by the hairstyle. But, sometimes when I'm all stiff getting out of the car after a long drive, I forget that the girl I once was is still there inside me. It's nice to remember that.

Straight Talk from the Barcalounger: Less Said, the Better

Ida wanted me to say somethin' about getting older here, but as far as I'm concerned, the less said the better. Gettin' started in the morning, sure, it takes me longer to rev up. But once I do, it's pedal to the metal. Gotta pace myself, though, or so Ida keeps tellin' me.

You know what? I've developed a real appreciation for sitting. In fact, if I'm working and have to stop to talk to somebody, I scope out a place to sit, or, at the very least, lean against something. And when I get home from the mill, 'fore supper, the minute my butt hits the Barcalounger, I nod off.

I don't know. I guess the biggest thing 'bout getting older is how it makes me keep a third eye out for folks who are even longer in the tooth than I am. It's not just walkin' slower when I'm with 'em, talkin' louder and looking out for the tippy factor. (My father-in-law's knees are wonky as all get out, even with shots of what he calls "WD-40.") It's paying attention when they're tellin' stories.

When I was a kid, hanging out with my granddad was borin', you know? He'd go on and on 'bout stuff that happened before I was born—stuff I didn't give a hoot about. Man, I wish I'd have listened more back then. So I'm listening now. Ida's dad has some real corkers. Not all of 'em I'd share with my wife!

Old-Man Feet

The other day, I saw Charlie in the bathroom checking out the hair in his ears and nose.

"Time for the Roto-Rooter?" I ask.

"Very funny," he replies. Then I hear him mutter under his breath, "If I could only get it to grow like this up top."

It's nice to know us women aren't the only ones who spend time thinking about how we're aging. Yet, I'm always surprised when Charlie seems concerned about it. I don't think of him as being that aware of how he looks, but I guess he is.

Like when we're talking about a celebrity or politician, or someone we just met at a party, and Charlie gets all wistful and says, "He sure has a good head of hair."

Every once in a while I catch him staring at his earlobes in the mirror to see if they're getting bigger.

A while back, Charlie and me are in the den, watching the tube. We're sitting in our Barcalounger love seat. It's in the semi-reclining position, so our feet are raised. Charlie has no socks on, and I notice he has a funny look of concentration on his face.

"What's a matter, dear," I says. "You got gas?"

"No," he sighs. "I was contemplating my toes. I'm starting to get old-man feet. See that? My toenails are turning yellow. And the nails on my big toes are beginning to tent up."

"Well, Charlie, if it'll make you feel any better, I'll show you my bunion."

Moose Teeth

My father-in-law André, who owned a gas station in Mahoosuc Mills and was one heck of a mechanic, used to say, "You put enough miles on her, and the wheels start to fall off."

As you grow older, your parts wear out. It can't be helped. Comes with the territory.

That's why it is a blessing that your eyesight is not as sharp as it once was, 'cause after a certain age some things you shouldn't

70

see up close. In fact, if you never had to ever see 'em, you could die happy. A while back, I had the dubious pleasure of gazing upon one of these things: color photographs of my back teeth.

Technology is part of the problem, of course. I mean, just 'cause it is possible to see your back teeth up close doesn't mean you should. Like the photos of my colon the gastroenterologist sent me home with last year. What was I supposed to do with those? Make Christmas cards out of 'em?

Anyhoo, I bit the bullet and went to the dentist. I confess, it had been a year. I was due. It was time to check out the place since old Dr. Ryder retired.

Dr. Ryder and me went way back. He was kind of old-school. He reminded me of André, trying to save you money.

> It is a blessing that your eyesight is not as sharp as it once was, 'cause after a certain age some things you shouldn't see up close.

"I could put a crown on it, Ida, but I think there's enough tooth for us to get by with a filling. It'll be a big one, but it's on a molar, so no one will notice."

Sometimes Dr. Ryder's technique was also like a car mechanic's. He'd jam his hands in your mouth, trying to strong-arm something into place. I'd hear Patty, his assistant, saying in the background, "Easy, Dr. Ryder. There's a person attached to that mouth."

Well, you should see the place now. This young fella, Dr. Dorfman, has taken over and redone the whole practice— painted the walls, added new carpet, hung jazzy artwork, and, of course, installed the latest equipment. And, since there's dental school to pay for, he's big on selling you his "treatment plan."

> *Area of concern? I'm thinking, You bet I'm concerned! How did those big yellow moose teeth get in my mouth?*

I suspect that's how they're training 'em these days. I've seen some of Dr. D's work. He's an artist the way he matches tooth color and size. Plus I've heard he's real gentle.

Thank goodness Becky the hygienist is still there. What a sweetheart! She did the X-rays and that gum-poking thing, which I hate, and she always makes me promise I'll floss religiously from that day forward, not "intermittently" like I normally do. I floss more than Charlie, though. I swear, he flosses one week a year. When I see him flossing in the bathroom, I go, "Dentist appointment coming up?"

Anyway, after the gum prodding, Becky did her scraping and polishing thing. Then she said, "I'm going to take pictures of your teeth so you can see what I'm looking at."

"Okay," I says, a little nervous.

Becky had this little camera on the end of a flexible cord, and she fooled around in my mouth with it, snapping shots, and recording them on her computer. (Gone are the little paper charts with illustrations of teeth. Now it's all there on the monitor, right in front of you.) Then, she showed me the pictures. Boy oh boy, was I ever shocked! Unlike an X-ray where it's hard to make out what you're seeing, with the photos you're actually looking at your teeth, up close and personal.

"See how this molar is mostly filling, and there's a bit broken off there?" Becky says. Then, "You can see here where you have two teeth with different kinds of fillings almost butting up against each other. And it looks like there's a hairline crack, right here. This is an area of concern, Ida."

Area of concern? I'm thinking, You bet I'm concerned! How did those big yellow moose teeth get in my mouth? My front teeth are normal size and pretty good-looking. (I use them whitening strips.) But apparently in the back I have big, yellow moose teeth, with fillings that are hanging on for dear life.

Those photos are a great sales tool, though. I couldn't sign up for my "treatment plan" fast enough. For only, get this— $10,000! Can you believe it? But we're going to chip away at it, bit by bit. We start Phase One in January. I'm thinking a couple teeth a year for five years, and I'll have a movie-star mouth in no time. It won't be attached to a movie-star body, of course, but what can you do?

Old in Mahoosuc Mills Is . . .

- The blue tarps Whitey Hebert uses to cover up his permanent yard sale.
- The gristmill out on the River Road, built in 1821 and abandoned. Makes a good necking spot for teenagers, if memory serves.
- Ninety-nine-year-old Yvette LaBlanche. She lives in Evergreen Nursing Home. Her best friend, Florence Albert, is ninety-eight. Both of 'em only talk gibberish at this point, though Yvette sounds like she's talking French, and Florence, like she's speaking Yiddish. Still, they understand each other perfectly and get on like a house afire.
- Saying, "Is it hot enough for you?" or "Enough snow for you?" or "You can't get there from here."

73

- How do you make something old? Add an "e" or two. As in: Ye Olde Cobbler, The Candy Shoppe, Ye Olde Mill Restaurant and Gift Shoppe.

Berry Nice

I spent a little over eighty dollars on lipstick. Really! And I'm over the moon happy about it, too!

See, I've been wearing the same shade of lipstick for years: "Berry Nice." (Who comes up with these names, anyways?) It's the perfect shade of lipstick for me: not too red, not too orange, not too pink. It's just, well, Berry Nice!

Oh, I've experimented with other colors over the years, but they never quite measure up. They might look good in the store. (I confess, if they don't have a tester, sometimes I break the seal and try it on my hand.) But when I get the lipstick home and try it on for real: disaster! I either look washed out, or my skin seems kind of sallow. Or the color's too hard. Something! It's just a waste of money. Best to stay with what works.

So about a month ago, when I went to the Rite Aid in town and saw that there was no Berry Nice in the rack, I felt a little flutter in my tummy. I check back the next week—still no Berry Nice. I usually keep a few tubes of Berry Nice on hand, you know, one in my makeup bag, one in my pocket book, and another emergency back-up. By week three, I was down to my last tube of Berry Nice. Things were getting serious! I tried going to the Rite Aid in Dover-Foxcroft and the one in Dexter—no Berry Nice. I was thinking about just throwing myself on my mascara wand and ending it all.

My last hope was Bangor. So when I suggested to Charlie that we go to the big city for a date night, maybe have dinner at the Olive Garden, I had an ulterior motive. Charlie went for it, though, 'cause he wanted to go to Home Depot and browse the tool department. They had a sale going on and Charlie was looking for some new gadget or other.

So I ask Charlie to stop at the Rite Aid when we get into Bangor.

"No need to come in. I'll just be a minute."

I go in, bee-lining it for the cosmetic section, ever hopeful. When I see that lonesome, empty spot in the rack where the Berry Nice is supposed to be, my heart sinks.

"Can I help you find something?" the sales clerk asks me, looking cute as a button.

"Yes, I'm looking for some Berry Nice lipstick, but there's none in the rack."

"Gee," she says, "I think that's been discontinued." The panic must have shown on my face, because she goes, "We just pulled a bunch of stuff to send back to the manufacturer. I can check and see if there's any still in the storeroom."

"Would you? Please?" I know I sounded desperate, 'cause I was. Off she went to check, and I closed my eyes said a quick little shopping prayer to my dearly departed mother.

I just hate it when things I like get discontinued, don't you? A special moisturizer, body wash, a style of bra. You know what it does? It makes me feel old and unpopular, like I'm not keeping up with the times. I was starting to feel a little sorry for myself when my sales clerk returned.

"Found some out back!" she says. "The color's been discontinued, but we haven't shipped them out yet."

"Thank God! How many tubes do you have?"

"Ten."

"I'll take 'em."

"All ten?"

"As many as you got!"

So, that's how I come to spend little over eighty dollars on lipstick. And boy, did I have a bounce in my step as a left the store!

"Find what you needed?" Charlie asks.

"Yes, as a matter of fact, I did." (No need to go into details.)

Crisis averted, temporarily, at least. But it'll buy me time to get used to the idea of finding a new lipstick color. 'Til then, everything's berry nice!

Gentle Yoga

Trying new things is a key to aging gracefully—you know, trying a new lipstick color or nail polish, brushing your teeth with the other hand, taking up a new hobby, learning a second language, and so forth. So last Saturday morning, I took a yoga class with Caitlin. She's been bugging me for ages to go with her, and finally I figured now's as good a time as any.

Besides, yoga's supposed to improve your strength, flexibility, and balance. And, frankly, at this point, I need to take precautions so's I won't fall down and break something.

I ate a light breakfast that morning. Didn't want to be too logy for class. Besides, I figured we could drop by the Busy Bee after for one of Babe's famous cinnamon rolls with maple icing. To die for!

> *"Oh, Caitlin, I just couldn't stomach the idea of using some mat other people've sweated on. Honey, there's not enough Purell in the world!"*

Caitlin picks me up a little before nine. "Gee, Aunt Ida," she says, "don't you look cute. Your outfit even matches your yoga mat."

"Got 'em both down to the Wally Mart the last time I was there; as you know, sky blue is pretty prominent on my color book," I says.

"I do. It's one of your star colors. You didn't need to buy a mat, though. I told you, they have 'em there at the yoga studio."

"Oh, Caitlin, I just couldn't stomach the idea of using some mat other people've sweated on. Honey, there's not enough Purell in the world!"

"Then you'd better bring a blanket, too. You'll need it for Corpse pose. We do that at the end of the class."

"Corpse pose? How hard does this gal plan to work us? 'Til we keel over?"

"Oh, no, Aunt Ida! Nothing like that."

"You know, as a rule, I try not to break a sweat."

"I know. Not to worry. This is a gentle yoga class. It's all about going at your own pace, not forcing anything. You're gonna love it!"

So we get to the yoga studio, and it's real nice: a big open room, New Agey music playing, incense burning, the works. Everyone's talking in hushed tones.

Then the teacher—this slender woman, probably in her late thirties—rings a bell and the class begins. She starts by introducing herself. Turns out she has some kind of spiritual name, although I can't remember now what it was. All I know is that it sounded like a healthy breakfast. You know, one of them all-natural, high-fiber cereals with fruit. "Kashi" or "Kashi-

I was fond of the Corpse pose, too, as it turns out. That consists of lying on your back with a blanket over you, thinking about warm cinnamon rolls with maple icing. Sorry! That last part was what I was doing, while the rest of the class was lying there thanking their bodies for a job well done.

Banana," or something like that. She calls herself a yogi. Says she's been practicing for . . . I don't know how long, 'cause at this point all I can picture is Yogi Bear eating some cereal he's stolen from a camper in Jellystone Park.

We just get started when I feel this giggling fit coming on (this used to happen to me at Mass sometimes), and I'm trying not to let it out. Then I start overheating. I mean, waves of warmth, radiating up. By now the class is concentrating on breathing in and out, in and out, and it sounds just like a Darth Vader group meeting. Suddenly, I let a burst of laughter escape, more like a snort, actually, a really loud snort. I just couldn't help it.

Kashi-Banana doesn't miss a beat.

"Yes," she says, "feel free to vocalize in any way that moves you. Let it out."

Then I can see Caitlin out of the corner of my eye, and she's starting to lose it, too. Tears are streaming down my face. I feel like I'm going to pass out! Not to mention, of course, I have to pee. What a workout! And we weren't even five minutes into the class.

It was hard, but after doing a little "centering" in the ladies' room, I managed to pull myself together. I scurry back to class and do the whole menagerie: the Up Dog, Down Dog, Cat, Cow, Cobra, Frog, Camel, and the One-legged Pigeon thrown in for good measure. And I kept the giggling to a minimum, too, except when someone let it rip during the Wind-Relieving pose. Well, how could I not? To be fair, I wasn't the only one who cracked up.

Kashi-Banana was pretty low-key, let me tell you. She'd say things like, "I invite you to relax and breathe into the stretch, honoring your body, never doing more than what feels right."

I can't say how much of the class "felt right," but it wasn't bad. Kind of relaxing, really. My favorite pose might have been the Mountain, which is basically just standing there. I was fond of the Corpse pose, too, as it turns out. That consists of lying on your back with a blanket over you, thinking about warm cinnamon rolls with maple icing. Sorry! That last part was what I was doing, while the rest of the class was lying there thanking their bodies for a job well done.

Okay, the hardest part of yoga class? Getting up from that darned Corpse pose! Lying on the floor for ten minutes is easy, but I got to say, once you get to a certain age, getting up from that position ain't much to look at, if you catch my drift. Especially if there's nothing to grab onto.

"Go ahead, Caitlin," I says, rolling over onto all fours, "leave me here. Save yourself!"

"Come on, Aunt Ida," she replies. "I believe there's a cinnamon roll with your name on it down to the Busy Bee."

Candid Camera

When it comes to aging gracefully, it's important to keep your morale up. You have to remember that fluorescent lights in a ladies' room make everyone look bad. Use your magnifying mirror sparingly, and do not look at your whole face at one time—just parts of it. And, absolutely, no candid photos ever. Don't take 'em. I don't want to see them.

The other day I had the misfortune of seeing some photos taken at our New Year's Day brunch at Celeste and Bud's. Rita got a new iPhone for Christmas, and, while I'm happy for her, it was like spending the day with the paparazzi.

Posed shots are okay because you have time to assemble your parts and put them where you want them. You wedge yourself

> *Everyone else in those pictures looks just like they do in real life. What's up with that? How come it's only me that looks older?*

between a couple of friends and turn sideways. That makes you look thinner. Then you suck in your gut and do the Princess Diana bit. You know, tilt your head down a little and look up. This kind of camouflages whatever double-chin action you got going. And you smile, of course, which lifts up the corners of your eyes and your whole face, really. Those shots pass muster.

But candids—whoa, Nellie! Unlike a moose, who always looks pretty impressive in impromptu photos, I do not: eyes half-closed in mid-sentence, or a profile shot of me in all my post-holiday, un-Spanxed glory, turkey neck and all. There was one photo where, I swear, I looked like Jabba the Hutt. I kid you not. Granted, the couch I was sitting on was very low and needed to be restuffed, so I was kind of scrunched down, but still, it's just so discouraging.

See, I have an image of myself in my head that is definitely cuter and about ten or even twenty years younger than I am in those photos. I'm not conceited or nothing, and I hope I'm not alone on this, but most of the time, even when I look in the mirror, I don't really see me. My mind kind of fills in the lines, if you know what I mean. It airbrushes my reflection, softens it. I don't feel my age, so I don't really see my age. Which is a good thing, because if I started feeling like I looked in Rita's snapshots, it would be hard to get out of bed in the morning. (The weird thing is, everyone else in those pictures looks just like they do in real life. What's up with that? How come it's only me that looks older?)

So Saturday night, Charlie and me were down to the Brew Ha-Ha. It was *Hee Haw* Night, and they were playing reruns of the old TV show on the big flat-screen over the bar. Everyone was country line dancing. Oh, it was a lot of fun! I wore my powder-blue Western shirt and a blue bandana with sunflowers on it 'round my neck.

So, I'm in the ladies', powdering my nose and fluffing up my hair, thinking, Gee, I'm looking pretty cute tonight, so much better than in them pictures of Rita's. I'm feeling perky as I turn to leave, a little bounce in my step. Then my right knee goes out. That's the one that's been bothering me lately. I didn't fall down or nothing. It just kind of seized up. Darn! It's God giving me the old reality check again, and all I can do is chuckle as I kind of hobble my gimpy way back to our table.

The number-one key to aging gracefully? Having a sense of humor, of course. You gotta laugh, or you'll cry.

Savor the Pause

I don't know about you, but time has changed as I get older. It feels like I'm living in a time warp! It's like some crap episode of Star Trek, where time's slows down when I wish it'd go faster, and speeds up when I want to linger.

Here's what I mean:

I'm getting my teeth cleaned, right? And the hygienist is doing that part where they poke around at your gums. I'm staring into the light just past her head, trying to go to my happy place. Instead, I'm sucked into this slow as molasses, grandfather clock, tick-tock, pick-poke zone thinkin' is she ever gonna finish?

Or, I'm getting ready to go away for the weekend with Charlie. We're gonna head down the coast for a second hon-

eymoon, leave Friday, right after work. The big day arrives.
I've set aside some time before my shift down to the A&P to
pack. Well, things start off normal enough, but then the situation gets wonky. Every time I glance at the clock, it's five, ten,
fifteen minutes later than I think it should be. The closer it gets
to when I have to leave, the quicker time's flying by. Finally, I
reach the tipping point where I know there's no way I'm gonna
get it all done before I have to go to work. Which means a
time crunch later, throwing my clothes and stuff all willy-nilly
into my suitcase, then rushing around the house, pulling things
together while Charlie waits in the car with the engine running!

I don't remember time ever being like this in my twenties,
thirties, ore even forties. When I was a kid, sure. Time would
speed up when I was playing, or right before I had to go to
bed, then slow down again when I was sitting in school waiting
for the bell to ring. Or I'd be squirming in the pew at church
wondering if we were getting close to communion, 'cause that
meant mass was almost over.

But this speeding up and slowing down of time in my youth
was a gentler, more reliable thing, almost like breathing—
expanding and contracting, expanding and contracting.

Now, time feels more like a slinky, unpredictable and unde-
pendable. One minute, I have a hold of it. The next, time's
tumbling down the stairs, end over end, picking up speed, then
slamming to a full stop at the bottom.

It's that full stop that's become more alluring the older I
get. I can't control the time warp, but I can accept and savor
the pause: a nap, a cup of tea with the latest issue of the Oprah
magazine. Taking a minute to scratch Scamp's belly or kiss the
top of Charlie's head. The full stop is a gift. I'm not cursing time

for going too fast, or wishing it away 'cause it's going so slow. I'm here lingering in the pause, for as long as it lasts.

Gettin' Going

- Suffering with menopause symptoms? Need to find a good physical therapist? Looking to upgrade your moisturizer? Ask a friend or two for recommendations. There's no need to suffer, and it's nice to know you're not alone.
- Get yourself a good sunscreen and wear it.
- Try something new. Brush your teeth with your other hand. Take a yoga class. Pick out a new lipstick or nail polish color.
- Write down three answers to the following question: What do you know now that you didn't know then? Ask your husband and friends the same question. We really are wiser.
- Remember to laugh.
- Make aging gracefully a priority. Accept where you're at. Then, do the best you can with what you've got.
- Savor the pause.

Five

Tending Your Roots

A moose calf is born in the spring or early summer, and stays with its mother for a year. During that time, the moose mom teaches the calf how to survive, and does her best to protect it from danger. Then, come the following spring, she drives that yearling off so she can nurture the new calf that's coming. I'm thinking it must be confusing as all get out for the yearling, but eventually he moves on and learns to fend for himself. Trust me—I know a few parents with kids in their early twenties still living at home who could learn a thing or two from the moose in this regard.

When I think about living the good life, I imagine myself surrounded by family and friends. They're what keeps me grounded, or "centered," as Caitlin would say. They get my jokes, and love me even when I'm cranky and outta sorts. They make me laugh, encourage me to try new things, and tease me when I don't want to. And when the chips are down, I know they'll be there for me. If life is a tree, family and friends are the roots. I know I have to tend those roots in order for my tree to flourish.

I don't want you to get hung up on the word *family* here. I'm referring to whatever family means to you. It could be the family that you're born into, the family you married into, or the family you chose. Maybe it's you and your pet goldfish. It don't matter. Having family gives you a sense of belonging in this world, and no matter how often or how far you travel, you carry that feeling of home with you.

Made with Love

They say the kitchen is the heart of the home, and I believe that to be true.

This past spring, I baked up a batch of my grandmother's molasses cookies, and boy, they sure looked beautiful, if I do say so myself. Just like I remember.

I have Grammy's recipe written in her shaky hand on white (now yellowed) lined paper. The page even has Grammy's molasses stains on it. My mother had it laminated for me years ago, and I've used it so much it's starting to separate along the edges.

The thing I like most about this recipe is that in the margin at the top of the page, over "Old-Fashioned Drop Molasses Cookies," my grandmother has written, "<u>My best.</u>" Underlined, just like that. With a period, not an exclamation point. It was a statement of truth, not opinion.

Grammy used to make her molasses cookies like crazy around the holidays, and she'd give them away in fancy tins. But she always baked up a batch toward the end of March, beginning of April, too. Molasses cookies are a cold-weather dessert, so these end-of-winter cookies had a special meaning. They were a signal that spring was around the corner; that we wouldn't have molasses cookies again until October. So, as crocuses poked their hopeful green heads up between dwindling patches of snow, I tried once again to follow Grammy's lead.

Her recipe yields about sixty cookies, so making them takes a long time. I've tried cutting the recipe in half, but it doesn't work. It calls for "sour milk," or "buttermilk," or "regular milk to which vinegar has been added." And after you mix it up, you have to "let it stand 1 hr."

But here's the deal: While the cookies smell like my Grammy's as they're cooking, they don't taste like hers. I've always wondered why.

It's the same with "Mom's Dessert." This is a treat my father's mother, who we called "Mom," used to make. Not only is it delicious, but it's easy as all get out.

You just whip up some cream and add Hershey's Syrup to it for flavor. Then you take the chocolate whipped cream and slather it over both sides of a graham cracker. Do the same to another one, and stick it to the first, with the crackers standing on end. Keep frosting and sticking graham crackers together to form a loaf. Once the loaf is completed, you frost the outside of it with more chocolate whipped cream, and put it in the fridge to sit overnight. The next day, decorate your creation with some multicolored sprinkles and serve. The graham crackers absorb the whipped cream and you end up with this dense, rich, chocolaty dessert, which is good, but not as tasty as when Mom made it.

Now, I think I know why the baked chicken or roast pork of today don't taste like my grandmothers'. The animals are raised different, and they put I-don't-want-to-know-what into the

> *Maybe my taste buds have changed, and nothing's ever going to taste as good as it used to. Maybe those desserts tasted better 'cause someone else made 'em, or because in my child's mind, they were all wrapped up in love.*

feed. Even the organic meat Caitlin gets don't taste like what I remember, though it's closer.

But dessert ingredients are basically the same, right? I mean, flour is flour. Whipped cream is, well, heavenly, and Hershey's Syrup can't have changed that much. Still, I can follow these recipes to the letter, and please everyone, but to me—it's just not the same. To me, these goodies taste more like the memory of Grammy's molasses cookies or Mom's dessert: almost, but not quite—like the full flavor is just out of reach.

Maybe my taste buds have changed, and nothing's ever going to taste as good as it used to. Maybe those desserts tasted better 'cause someone else made 'em, or because in my child's mind, they were all wrapped up in love.

Still, how wonderful it is to have those memories.

Creating family traditions—whether it's bakin' cookies, chopping down your own Christmas tree, or watching a favorite TV show together—feed the roots of your family tree. And no one can take that feeling of being firmly planted away from you. Even when part of your family is no longer there.

Friendship in Mahoosuc Mills Is . . .

- The Card Sharks down to the bean supper at the Congo Church. That's a group of old-timers who arrive an hour early to make sure they get the seat they want and first dibs at the dessert table. While they're waitin', they play cards, and God help anyone who tries to cut ahead of 'em in line.

- The Women Who Run with the Moose. Heck, we've been together since God was in diapers! We finish each others sentences, and sometimes get laughing so hard, we pee our pants. If that's not friendship, I don't know what is.
- Something we don't take lightly. 'Cause when the chips are down, well, who else can you count on?

Live Every Day Like It's Your Last

I have great memories of Thanksgiving, and most of them involve my mother in an apron doing just about everything.

Oh, my dad would help her get the turkey into and out of the oven, and he'd carve. He'd cut up the turnip, too: a job for a man and maybe his chain saw. My sister Irene and me would peel the potatoes and stuff the celery with cream cheese, sprinkling a little paprika on top. But my mother did all the rest.

Mom kept a little notebook for as long as I can remember, with details about every holiday we celebrated. You could look up Thanksgiving 1967 and see how much turkey cost per pound, how big that turkey was, who was there, what the weather was like—you name it.

"Molded cuisine," Caitlin calls it. Nobody actually likes the salad, but we all put a little on our plate. Dad usually takes a bite out of loyalty to Mom.

Mom would set the table the day before, and get out all the serving dishes. In each dish, she'd put the serving spoon beside a little piece of paper with *sweet potatoes,* or *cranberry sauce,* or *rolls,* or *stuffing* written on it. She didn't want to forget something in the rush to get everything on the table.

Then my mom got cancer.

That first Thanksgiving, she was so sick from the radiation, Irene and me knew it would be too much for her to cook. We fretted about it for weeks. Finally, we worked up the courage to ask Mom if she minded if us girls cooked. I still remember the look of relief on her face. So, Irene and me cooked dinner together at Mom and Dad's house. We let Mom make the gravy, though you could tell she was itchin' to do more. That's what we did for the next three years as our mother suffered through recurrence after recurrence, operation after operation, more and more medication, 'til she finally just wasted away.

Mom died at home, surrounded by her family. It may sound strange unless you've experienced it, but being with her when she died was a beautiful thing.

The year after my mother died, Charlie and I hosted Thanksgiving at our house, and to be honest, I really didn't enjoy it. Our double-wide just ain't wide enough. People were jammed into the kitchen making gravy, carving the turkey, mashing the potatoes, mixing the carrot and turnip medley, checking on the butternut squash, and putting baby peas in a white sauce into those little puff-pastry shells. Everyone was frantic to get it all done at the same time—too stressful. Ever since that first year, we've had Thanksgiving at Irene's, and I help out. That's my favorite part now: puttering around the kitchen and giggling with Irene.

Irene says, "Ida, whatever you do, don't forget to make the Jell-O mold salad." That's one of the things we giggle about. I do the Jell-O mold salad at Thanksgiving because I inherited the mold that's shaped like a turkey. Irene makes it at Christmas in the wreath-shape mold.

Mom's Jell-O mold salad is the easiest thing in the world to make. It's just Jell-O, of course, fruit cocktail, miniature marsh-mallows, cream cheese, and Cool Whip. "Molded cuisine," Caitlin calls it. Nobody actually likes the salad, but we all put a little on our plate. Dad usually takes a bite out of loyalty to Mom.

I don't think she made up the recipe, but at some point Mom wrote it down on a piece of yellow lined paper, which by now is full of orange Jell-O stains smudging out some of the words. Truth be told, I know the recipe by heart, but I still get it out and put it on the counter. It's the weirdest thing. I can see pho-tos of my mother and it affects me, but not as much as seeing her handwriting in the margin of a book or on a recipe. That gets me. It's tangible proof that she was here.

But so is the sound of my voice when I open the oven and say, "How's Tom Turkey doing?" And the way Irene looks standing at the kitchen sink with her apron on, peeling potatoes; the hitch in my dad's voice as he's saying grace before dinner, and the pride in his eyes as he looks at us all gathered 'round the table.

A terminal illness, car accident, or even something good, like a vacation or the birth of a grandchild, really puts your priorities in order. It makes you appreciate things you've stopped seeing in the daily hustle and bustle. Live each day as if it could be your last, 'cause you never know, right?

No Regrets: Say It, and Let It Go

When Mom was sick, Dad, Irene, and me had a little thing we kept saying: "No regrets." We felt that grieving was going to be hard enough without adding regrets. If a little voice in our head said, "Call the doctor and ask him if we can do something more about the pain," we called. If Mom mentioned how she'd like to go strawberry-picking, off we went. A lobster dinner? Sure!

Talking to Mom about her life, telling her what a great mother she was, asking her if she was scared to die—it wasn't always easy to have those conversations, but in the long run, it's a heck of a lot better than carrying around a truckload of regrets.

If you want to live the good life, regrets definitely get in the way. So anything you can do to head 'em off at the pass, go for it.

Makes me think of a conversation I had with Dottie a while back. She was having some family trouble. Her brother, Frank, was drinking too much, and she was real worried about him. Dottie didn't want to confront him, though. "He'll stop talking to me," she says. But you could tell she was all balled up about it.

"Listen, Dottie, are you having meaningful conversations with him now?"

"No."

"Well, geez, what if he got in a car accident on his way home from the Brew Ha-Ha and died or something? How would you feel if you'd never confronted him about his drinking?"

"I'd never forgive myself."

"So, you've got nothing to lose, right? Talk to him! But don't get your hopes up. He probably won't quit drinking."

"Then what's the point, Ida?"

"The point, Dottie, is no regrets. At least you'll know in your heart that you did what you could. Your conscience will be clear. Say it, and let it go. It's out of your control."

 Caitlin's New Age Nook: Regrets Repair Remedy
Do you have something you wish you'd said to someone, but didn't or couldn't? Is there something you wish you'd done or didn't do? Having trouble letting it go? Try this exercise. It also works for getting rid of resentments.

You'll need some writing paper, a pen, and a quiet place to write, as well as matches or a lighter and a receptacle for burning paper.

Take a moment to get centered and connect with your breathing. When you feel present, pick up your pen and write. Don't think too hard about it—just stream-of-consciousness writing, beginning with the words "I regret" or "I resent," and continuing from there. You may have just one thing you want to clear, or many. Write until you come to a natural stopping point, or set a timer and write as much as you can within the allotted time.

Now, take what you've written, tear it into pieces, and burn it. As the paper disintegrates, enjoy the sense of release you feel as your regret/resentment goes up in smoke.

To close, shut your eyes and connect with your breathing once again. When you feel centered, open your eyes, pick up the pen and write, stream of consciousness, beginning with the words, "I forgive." If you're clearing a resentment, that forgiveness may be directed toward another, but when it comes to regrets, it's you you have to forgive. When you've written all you can, repeat the burning ritual, enjoying the sense of serenity and wholeness that comes from forgiveness.

It's important to not keep what you've written. Holding on to it is holding on to your regret. As Aunt Ida says, it's all about saying it and letting it go.

 ### Aunt Ida Tweaks It

This is a great exercise, but not everyone is comfortable writing, and then there's the chance you might set off the smoke alarms in your house.

I've tried this riding around in my car. I set aside some time for a drive, and, while by myself in the car,

I say what I wish I'd said, or done, or I talk to the person I'm trying "to reach closure" with. I talk and cry and talk some more 'til I'm all talked out. This works for people who are gone, but also for saying things (like to your sister-in-law or coworker) that you'd like to say, but know it would cause a world of hurt to unload on 'em. Then I go to the car wash. Seriously! As I'm sitting in my car and those big brushes set to work, I picture all those regrets, resentments, and any anger or sadness I've been feeling being scrubbed away. When I emerge into the sunlight, I feel like a new person. Plus, my car's clean. Win-win!

And Poodle Makes Three

When Charlie and me first got married, I had a hard time thinking of us as a family. Family still meant Mom, Dad, Irene, and me. But when Charlie and me found out that we couldn't have kids, we were forced to rethink "family." It took me a while to accept that a family could be just Charlie and me. Then we got our first dog, Belle, and our family became Charlie, me, and the dog.

Belle, a black standard poodle, was the best dog with the sweetest disposition and a heart of gold. To quote my friend, Mary, "If I can be half as good as Belle, I will die a happy woman." Belle went everywhere with me. She loved riding in the car, swimming, and if you threw a ball, she'd bring it back to you again and again and again. She never tired of it.

It's just amazing what unconditional love and no discipline whatsoever can accomplish! Now he rules the roost: fourteen pounds of joy wringing wet and cute as all get out.

Belle lead a good, full life, and when at fourteen she gave me the "it's time" look, it broke my heart. The next day, we brought her up to the lake for a swim (well, Charlie held her in the water), fed her some vanilla ice cream, and went to the vet. I swear, it was hardest thing Charlie and I have ever done!

It took about a month of walking into an empty house for me to start wanting another dog. You know, seeing that spot of the floor where Belle's bed used to be? I just missed having a little buddy. I like running errands, coming back to the car and seeing that head pop up in the window. I like having to get out and take a walk, regardless of the weather. Most of all, I like coming home and being greeted by someone who's over the moon happy to see me. Charlie is just not all that excitable.

When I started talking about a new dog, Charlie went along with it pretty quick. He knew how much I missed Belle. And to be honest, I think he was tired of me hugging him all the time, smelling the top of his head, scratching behind his ear saying in my talk-to-the-dog baby voice, "Who's the best husband in the whole wide world? I love you. Yes, I do!"

Lickity split, Pepper came into our lives. She was a brownish-beige cockapoo. What a love bug, and a total clown! When Pepper crossed the rainbow bridge, within a couple of weeks we brought home that rascal, Scamp.

Scamp's a bichon-poodle mix. He's 12 now, and has really mellowed out since he first arrived, shaking and skittish, from Poodle Rescue. It's just amazing what unconditional love and no discipline whatsoever can accomplish! Now he rules the roost: fourteen pounds of joy wringing wet and cute as all get out.

Having a pet is a great way to create a sense of family. Plus, they help to lower stress, and in the case of a dog, they get you out for a walk at least once a day. Or they should, anyway.

I don't start cashiering down to the A&P until eleven, but Charlie has to get up early for work. So I do Scamp's afternoon walk, and Charlie's got the morning shift. Usually, the drill is as follows:

Around six in the morning, Charlie hauls his butt out of bed and heads off to the bathroom. Then, half dressed, he pulls back the curtains over the kitchen sink, squints at the outdoor thermometer, and grunts. During the winter, this is followed by much layering on of under- and outerwear, punctuated by even more grunts and exhalations.

Even with the bedroom door closed, Scamp hears all this and sits right at the door, staring attentively at the doorknob. When Charlie opens the door, Scamp races out of the bedroom, eager to go outside for his morning constitutional.

Last winter, though, I started sensing a mounting reluctance on Scamp's part to leave the bedroom. All of a sudden, Scamp was no longer waiting by the door. He just stayed in his bed. Charlie would open the door, call for Scamp, and he wouldn't come.

"What the hell?" grumbles Charlie. "Scamp! Time for a walk!"

No movement. Finally, Charlie had to come in, grab Scamp, and haul him out of there.

A few mornings later, Charlie comes into the room to get Scamp, and he's not on his bed.

I'm laying there with my eyes closed, thinking about the day to come, when I hear Charlie whispering, "Scamp! Come here, boy! Scamp? Where are you?"

I open my eyes a crack. "Did he sneak out of the room?"

"Nope," says Charlie. "I heard his nails on the floor. I think he's hiding."

"Hiding?"

It's 6:15 in the morning, and Charlie and me are searching the bedroom for Scamp. We peek under the bed, and there he is, shaking.

"Scamp! What are you carrying on about? Don't you want to go for a walk?"

There's Charlie in full winter gear, including them big Sorel boots and his hat with the earflaps, and me in my nightgown, on the floor, trying to coax our little drama queen into going outside for a walk! He's a dog, for God's sake!

After several mornings of this nonsense, we came up with a solution. The technique that seems to work best is for me to pretend I'm leaving the bedroom. When Scamp follows, I scoop him up before he can head back under the bed and hand him to Charlie. So much for my thinking time! By then, heck, I'm up and the day's begun. That little bugger!

Of course, once Scamp's outside, he isn't cold. He just loves the snow, and Charlie can hardly keep up with him.

God, Scamp makes me laugh! For me, having a pet is an important part of living the good life.

Choosing Family

I know they say, "You can't choose your family." But I say, "Why not?" Family, like life, is what you make it. The traditional family pretty much died with Eisenhower (though we keep pretending). So, you have the freedom of cherry-picking who you want as your family. Spending Thanksgiving with friends is a great way to create a sense of family. Or having a buddy you consider a sister, or an aunt who feels like a mother. Put energy into creating an "A-Team" of a family and you'll reap big rewards: love, support, and a sense of belonging.

Now, I'm not saying you should (or can) cut off all ties to your biological family. That's just not practical for most people (though for some it's the only way, a matter of survival). It's about changing how you think about them, and how you choose to spend your time.

I have a friend, let's call her Sally, who looks at spending time with family as "service work."

> I know they say, "You can't choose your family." But I say, "Why not?" Family, like life, is what you make it. The traditional family pretty much died with Eisenhower (though we keep pretending). So, you have the freedom of cherry-picking who you want as your family.

"Being with my brother was always tough. We're just so different, and I don't agree with his choices," says Sally. "Whenever I spent time with him, I'd leave depressed. Then I had this revelation: I'd feel better about taking him to lunch if he was a complete stranger. Now I think of spending time with him as service work. It's like volunteering down to the soup kitchen or making cookies for the senior center. It's something I do to give back, and I don't expect anything in return. It's made a world of difference in how I feel about him and my whole family."

During the holidays, family time goes into overload. (Why isn't Thanksgiving in March when it would be nice to have a holiday, instead of so close to Christmas?) It's a busy time of year, and the demand for service work cranks up a notch. But remember: You may not be able to get out of spending Christmas with the family you were born into, but you don't have to spend the whole day there. Build in some time for you and your A-team family.

Come Hell or High Water

Whether you chose it, are born into it, or marry into it, no family's perfect. Every family has a certain way of doing things that may seem weird to others. Heck, it may seem weird to you, but it's just how you operate. You take pride in it or joke around about it.

Like a while back, we had a birthday brunch for our dad, over to Irene and Jimbo's. She made the "Egg Dish" (there's only one), which is something our mom used to make involving about a dozen eggs, butter, bread, milk, and cheese. How can you go wrong with that combo, right? You whip it up the night before, and the next morning it bakes up nice and light. I brought along some fruit salad and cranberry nut bread, and Jimbo fried up a whole mess of bacon. (As far as we're concerned, if there ever was a food of the gods, bacon is it.)

"So, I'm on my way to the book club, right? Hanging my arm out the car window, when somehow, it gets lopped off. But do I go to the emergency room?"

"You do not! You put a tourniquet on it and go to that book club."

"Yes, I do. 'I'm here,' I say. 'Just ignore the spurting blood, and tell me where to put these cookies.' "

Charlie and me picked up Dad from Mahoosuc Green. They'd already done a birthday celebration for him there on his proper birthday, which was Friday. Dad loves being surrounded by family; he's always teasing us and laughing. Somehow, though, he didn't seem his usual self. The minute he unwrapped his last present, he said, "All right, then," which is Dad's signal that he's ready to go. He does this on the phone, too. "All right, then," he said, and was in the truck before Charlie and me could get our coats on.

99

Later, Irene calls me. "I don't think Dad was feeling too good."

"No," I agreed. "He didn't even touch his bacon."

"That's bad."

I called Dad that evening, and he was sick in bed with some flu-type thing. Sounded awful, too. "*Mon Dieu!*" he says. "Been coming out of both ends."

"When did that start?"

"Last night."

"Jeez, Dad! Why did you come to brunch if you didn't feel good? We could have rescheduled."

"I wanted to see you girls, and I know you'd fussed. Besides, I made a commitment."

There you have it: our family in a nutshell. We have driven in blizzards to go to events that were canceled on account of the weather. It never occurs to us that someone might cancel something once it's planned. We show up "French early" to parties no matter what shape we're in: bad backs, headaches—don't matter. And usually we bring a hostess gift. If we say we're going to the gym or walking or out for lunch, you can bet dollars to donuts that we'll be there. I mean, the Apocalypse would have to be in full swing before we'd break a commitment. Yes, we are loyal and stubborn to a fault.

Me and Irene joke around about it. "So, I'm on my way to the book club, right? Hanging my arm out the car window, when somehow, it gets lopped off. But do I go to the emergency room?"

"You do not! You put a tourniquet on it and go to that book club."

"Yes, I do. 'I'm here,' I say. 'Just ignore the spurting blood, and tell me where to put these cookies.'"

100

The Social Network

They say that having a good social network helps us live longer. And I believe it! It certainly makes my life richer. Now, I'm not talking about Facebook or Twitter. I'm talking about friends. Making good, strong friendships a priority is an important part of living the good life. It really makes a difference even if you're married or in a relationship—especially if you're married or in a relationship. Here's the deal: A man will try to solve your problems; a girlfriend will just listen. And honey, sometimes that's all you want!

Of course, friendship, like anything else, takes time and energy. But it's worth the effort. One way I've found to make and maintain friendships is to have a standing date. It might be breakfast once a week, a monthly movie night, or a call every two weeks if someone lives far away. If you wait until you're thinking, "I haven't seen so-and-so for ages; I'm going to email her and ask her to lunch," it's going to be another three weeks before you can get together because you're both so busy. But when you're having lunch, if you say, "Let's put something on the calendar for next month," you know it's going to happen. This works for family, too. For example, I have breakfast with Irene once a week, and I call my dad every other day. Tend those roots!

The Women Who Run with the Moose have been doing this for years. Celeste, Rita, Betty, Dot, Shirley, and me get together once a week for a little girlfriend time—that's a given. But when it's one of our birthdays, we like to do something special; you know, mix it up a little.

Lately, we've been going to a spa in Bangor called the New You. It all started last winter when it was time to celebrate Dot's big day. (I'm sworn to secrecy about which milestone it was. Let's just say it ends in zero and Dottie's been a member of AARP for ten years. Poor dear.) She was a little down in the dumps about it, so we thought we'd perk her up with a field trip.

Winter is long up here in Mahoosuc Mills, whether we get a lot of snow or not. So Betty decided that we were all in need of a little pampering. Betty's always up on the latest stuff, and she'd heard of this New You Spa that was supposed to be real swanky. So we pile into Shirley's Bonneville and head for the big city, Bangor.

We all brought along a little nourishment to get us through the drive. I swear, there was enough chocolate in that car to make Willie Wonka jealous. But it was okay because we were just eating the dark chocolate, which is good for your heart.

> *I swear, there was enough chocolate in that car to make Willie Wonka jealous. But it was okay because we were just eating the dark chocolate, which is good for your heart.*

It took us forever to get to Bangor because we had to stop at every rest area. We believe that if you have the chance to go, go. You never know when the next bathroom opportunity might present itself. Our motto is: *Carpe Peeum*.

At the New You, us girls all chipped in and bought Dot the "mini-vacation" package, complete with a facial, seaweed wrap, and hot stone massage.

So they take Dot away for her pampering. Betty goes in for a massage and Shirley for her appointment. Shirley says, "I am not getting naked and letting some stranger touch me. It's just too intimate." So she was just getting a mani-pedi—that's a manicure and pedicure.

That left Celeste, Rita, and me to wander around the gift shop until it was our turn. I'd had a massage before, years ago, in Portland. It was a gift from Caitlin. So I decided to try something new and get what they call a "body polishing treatment." I figured, what the heck. I'm a little gem. Go for it!

So, when it's time for my appointment, Rita, Celeste, and me are sitting there, admiring Shirley's nails, when a man walks down the hallway to the waiting area. We all stop talking and stare. This fella is a hunk—tall and muscular, kind of looks like that soccer player who's married to the Spice Girl (the one who always looks so serious—probably 'cause she doesn't have any body fat to be truly happy). And when he smiles, I realize in my whole life I've never seen a man with teeth that white.

> So I get undressed, making sure to fold my clothes all nice and neat and hide my underwear underneath. Was I ever glad I shaved my legs that morning!

"Ida?" he says.

Shirley pokes me in the ribs.

"Uh, that's me," I reply.

"I'm Brad. I'll be giving you your body polishing treatment today."

I'm thinking, There is a God!

So, I follow Brad down the hall, my heart racing. When we get to the room, he says, "Please remove your clothes and get under the blanket. I'll be back in a few minutes."

So I get undressed, making sure to fold my clothes all nice and neat and hide my underwear underneath. Was I ever glad I shaved my legs that morning! So, I'm lying on the massage table in my birthday suit with a heated blanket on top of me, waiting for Brad.

There's a knock on the door and in walks Brad. He explains the drill in this calm, quiet voice like they do, and then asks, "Do you have any questions or concerns about today's treatment?"

"Brad, I'm putty in your hands. Let's get to it."

Brad smears my body with this stuff that's the consistency of the natural peanut butter Caitlin gets at the health food store. And then, I swear to God, he sanded me like I was a piece of wood.

After that, I go shower off the peanut butter stuff and get back on the table. Brad wraps me in hot towels to open my pores, puts cucumber slices on my eyes, and then, for the grand finale, he massages me with this natural moisturizer that smells like a Creamsicle. Was it ever heavenly! By the time my new best friend Brad was finished, my body was all pink and tingly and smooth as a baby's bottom. I'm thinking, Wait until Charlie gets a load of this!

Afterwards, my legs were so rubbery, I had to sit down to put my pants on! I wobbled out into the waiting room. All the girls turn toward me and smile.

Dot asks, "So, how was it?"

"Dottie, it was so good, I need a cigarette—and I don't even smoke!"

Then Shirley stands up, puts her hands on her hips, and goes, "That does it! It's my birthday next month, and I'm making an appointment with Brad."

Straight Talk from the Barcalounger: Need-to-Know Basis

The key to good friendships? Don't get too personal. Me and the boys operate on a need-to-know basis. We go fishing and hunting. We play poker and pool. Take a snowmobile trip every now and then. It's about having a good time and not dwelling on the personal stuff.

Ida's always asking what me and the boys talk about when we get together. I say "Nothing," and I'm telling the truth, though she seems skeptical. If pressed, I guess we talk about hunting, fishing, our gear. Oh, and the Sox, Patriots, Bruins. That's pretty much it.

I remember the last time me and Ida went to the Pilot's Grill. We were waiting in line and there's this couple ahead of us. Ida starts talking with the woman,

> *By the time we're seated, Ida knows everything about the couple: how they met, how many children they have, how many grandchildren—you name it. And me? I know jack about the guy. Which is fine by me, 'cause I don't care. I'm never going to see him again!*

while me and the guy stand there, discussing the weather.

It's amazing! In a matter of seconds, the girls are gabbing a mile a minute, like they are long-lost friends, even though they just met. By the time we're seated, Ida knows everything about the couple: how they met, how many children they have, how many grandchildren—you name it. And me? I know jack about the guy. Which is fine by me, 'cause I don't care. I'm never going to see him again!

Slaying Energy Vampires

Have you ever met a vampire? I'm not talking about them sexy bloodsuckers you see in movies and on TV nowadays. (Truth be told, those fellas make me wish I was more of a night person!)

No, I'm talking about energy vampires. You know, those so-called friends who take more than they give? The ones who never really listen (provided they even let you squeeze a word in edgewise). Given half a chance, these creatures'll just suck the life right out of you. Won't even think twice.

I remember this one time, a few years back. I was at the Knights of Columbus summer picnic, heading for the dessert table, when a "friend" (let's call her Myrtle) heads me off at the pass.

"Hey, Myrtle," I says, "how you doing?"

"Oh, Ida, not too good. Not too good at all."

Oh boy, here we go, I'm thinking. But I say, "Sorry to hear that, dear."

See, I'm trying to keep up my forward momentum 'cause there's some strawberry shortcake just a couple of steps away with my name on it, but Myrtle puts her hand on my arm, stopping me. Then she steps right up close to me and takes a deep breath, kind of like them Dementors in *Harry Potter*, and she's off.

"Pete and me aren't doing too well."

"I'm sorry to hear that." (Truth is, Pete and Myrtle have never been "doing too well," and frankly, I think that's the way Myrtle likes it.)

"I know we should probably give counseling a try, but really, do I want to try to save something that wasn't that good to begin with? Besides, where would I find the time? You know, my mother's living with us, and she's a handful, let me tell you. 'Course, everything would be easier if I had more energy. This Lyme disease."

"You got Lyme?"

"Yes! Well, my test come back negative, but I know I have it. Not that the insurance company would cover it if I did . . ."

She just goes on and on. Myrtle's like a Gatling gun. 'Bout all you can do is nod your head.

"And to top things off, Ida, I have this paper cut on my thumb that's driving me crazy! Throbs so. Keeps me up at night. Not that I get much sleep anyways, with Pete's snoring. I think he needs to see someone, a specialist or something. And—oh, there's Jeanie. I have to say hi. Nice talking to you, Ida!"

And off she goes in search of another victim. 'Course, at this point, she's bursting with energy: my energy.

I'm standing there, stunned, when Celeste happens by a few minutes later. "Ida, what is it?" she asks.

"Myrtle."

"Oh, honey, you need a big hug."

"And some strawberry shortcake," I whimper.

See, I'm positive and upbeat most of the time, and that's why they're drawn to me. Used to happen to me down to the A&P, too. Some days, I'd start to wondering if my register light read, ENERGY VAMPIRE CHECKOUT—FULL CARTS ONLY!

I don't know if it's menopause or what, but I finally decided I just wasn't going to put up with this kind of crap anymore. Spending time with friends should be energizing and fun. Sure, there'll be times when a friend is down in the dumps, or sick or something, and you're there for her, of course. Being there to support her makes you feel good, 'cause you know she'd do the same for you.

But when hanging out with a friend starts to seem like an obligation, something you have to get psyched up for, or if you consistently feel drained after getting together, I say it's time to take a hard look at that "friendship." You may be hanging out with an energy vampire.

The good thing is, you don't have to confront 'em. They wouldn't get what you're saying if you handed it to 'em on a silver platter. In order for them to see your point of view, they'd have to take responsibility for their behavior, and they're not about to do that.

So stop making the effort, stop trying to solve their problems, and move on. It's better to have one good, solid friendship than a bunch of these bloodsuckers draining you dry. Want to spend time with vampires? Catch 'em on the tube!

Caitlin's New Age Nook: Slaying an Energy Vampire

Need to banish an energy vampire? Blast them with love! Sounds counterintuitive, I know. But people like this are black holes, and they're drawn to your good energy. They feed off it. So, "Use the force, Luke." Picture a beam of pink light blasting out of your heart and surround them with it. Send them love, compassion, and bright light. Vampires are repelled by the light and will run away. Try it and you'll see.

This works if an energy vampire is hanging around someone you love, too. First, protect your loved one by visualizing yourself throwing a net of love over them, or surrounding them with a protective shield. Then blast that vampire with love.

Aunt Ida Tweaks It

Sounds kind of woo-woo, but you know what? I started doing it, and it works! In fact, I did some vampire blasting down to the bean supper at the Congo Church this past Saturday. Again, I won't name names, but not only did Charlie and me not have to sit with 'em, we got those two pieces of peanut butter pie we had our eyes on!

Gettin' Going

- Consciously decide to make family and friends a priority in your life. Do it now because you never know.

- Create a new family tradition: go berry picking, make pancakes together on Sunday morning, go bowling.
- Feeling lonely? Consider taking the plunge and getting a pet. You won't be sorry.
- If you didn't hit the jackpot in the family department, do something about it. Create your own holiday celebration. Make a list of your "A-Team" family. Experiment with the "service work" idea.
- Make a standing date with a friend or two.
- Take a good, hard look at your friends and banish the energy vampires. As anyone who has lived through high school knows, you become like the people you hang out with. Ask yourself: Are my family/friends cheerful? Do they have a positive outlook? Are they game to try new things? Do they make me laugh? Are they interested in me and what I'm doing? Surround yourself with people who love and support you and do the same for them. And your tree of life will flourish.

Six

A Good Marriage Starts with Please and Thank You

Charlie and me have been happily married for forty years. That don't make me an expert, but it gives me lots to talk about, relationship-wise.

When Caitlin and me were doing our research, there didn't seem like much we could learn from a moose regarding marriage. They tend to be solitary creatures. Don't hang around in a herd. Just come together in the fall for a little mating.

Then I saw a fact that caught my eye. During the mating season, male moose will sometimes get into a pushing match over a female. But they don't get too carried away, 'cause if they butt heads too hard, their antlers will lock, and they'll die. They have a pair of stuffed moose with locked antlers down to L.L. Bean, and it just breaks my heart.

Marriage is like that, too. If you don't compromise every now and then, if you're constantly butting heads, you're just not gonna make it as a couple. You gotta learn to pick your battles.

Other than that, my advice for having a happy marriage sounds a lot like what I'd tell a kid going to summer sleepaway camp:

• Always say please and thank you.

- Do your share of the chores.
- Wear clean underwear.
- If you mess up, 'fess up.
- And most important, have a good time!

High School Sweethearts

I can't remember a time when I didn't know Charlie—Mahoosuc Mills just isn't that big—though we only started dating in high school. That's right, we were high school sweethearts.

We got married two weeks after I graduated. He was a couple years older than me. Charlie graduated third in his class. 'Course, there was only six of them.

The day of our wedding, I promised myself I wouldn't shed a tear. I was doing pretty good, too, until I was just about ready to walk down the aisle. My father looked at me and said, "Ida, you're not my little girl anymore." That did me in. I cried the entire ceremony. Charlie looked so handsome in his white tux. The bridesmaids were all in different color pastels—one in pink, one in yellow—you know. My sister, Irene, was the maid of honor. I remember, she had on the prettiest periwinkle blue.

Charlie and me were a little giddy by the time we got to the reception over to the Fish and Game Hall. We'd drunk some champagne in the car. Let me tell you, those ushers tricked out Charlie's Dodge Dart within an inch of its life. Streamers, tin cans, JUST MARRIED written all over the windshield. The minute the photos were over, Charlie took off his shoes. The rented tux was okay, but the shoes were just too tight. The Fish and Game Hall looked wonderful. Me and the girls had decorated it with crepe paper and balloons. Even gussied up all the animal heads on the walls.

It seemed like all of Mahoosuc Mills was there. It was pot-luck, BYOB. That was pretty normal back then. You go that route, and the food's always good, 'cause people put in extra effort for a wedding. Kid Morensy set up his stereo and every-one brought their favorite records. Our first dance together as husband and wife was to Elvis singing "All Shook Up." Charlie's a hell of a dancer.

We were all drinking beer, laughing, and dancing up a storm. Charlie and me knew our marriage was official when Emile Dugall sang *"Prendre Un P'tit Coup."* Every wedding in town, the minute he'd get a buzz on, he'd sing the same song. And every-one joined in.

Prendre un p'tit coup, c'est agréable,
Prendre un p'tit coup, c'est doux.
Prendre un p'tit coup, ça rend l'esprit malade,
Prendre un p'tit coup, c'est agréable!
Prendre un p'tit coup, c'est doux!

(This is an old song. Hard to translate it into English, but this is the gist.)

Having a drink, feels great,
Having a drink, feels soothing.
Having a drink, makes your head spin,
Having a drink, feels great!
Having a drink, feels soothing!

After we cut the cake and fed each other a bite—I'd made Charlie promise he wouldn't smoosh it in my face—I changed into a pink suit and we left for our honeymoon: a long weekend on the coast of Maine. We didn't have much money at the time, and that's about all we could afford. We stayed in Damariscotta, though we could have been anywhere since we hardly left the hotel room.

R-E-S-P-E-C-T

One of the first things that attracted me to Charlie was his manners. He was always real polite, holding the door open for me like a gentleman and saying "please" and "thank you." I knew he'd been raised like I'd been.

To this day, we still say "please" and "thank you" to each other for even the smallest things.

"Thanks for mowing the lawn, Charlie."

"Ida, please pass me that cute little Mrs. Claus salt shaker you got down to the Christmas Tree Shops." (Well, I embellished that one a little, but you get the idea.)

> *And that's what marriage is all about: It's the give-and-take of building a life together, the shared memories, and making your relationship a priority.*

Saying please and thank you is a sign of respect, which, in my opinion, is probably the most important thing in a marriage. You might not have been raised in the same way or see eye to eye on everything, but if you respect each other, you have a starting point for discussion, which can lead to compromise. And that's what marriage is all about: It's the give-and-take of building a life together, the shared memories, and making your relationship a priority.

Caitlin's New Age Nook: Marry Yourself

Not in a relationship and feel like something is missing? Just out of a relationship and feeling a little lost? Putting off things (buying a house, taking a special trip) until you're with that special person? This ritual helped my friend, Jennifer, and it may help you feel more settled, too.

Marry yourself. Just think about it. Marriage is a ritual where you promise to love, honor, and respect. Renewing that commitment to yourself is a way of setting a powerful intention. And once you feel complete in yourself, you are more likely to attract a healthy, loving relationship. And in the meantime, your life is no longer on hold.

This ritual can be as simple or elaborate as you want. Write vows to yourself, buy yourself a symbol (like a ring) of your commitment to yourself, get some flowers, a special outfit. And don't forget to take yourself on a honeymoon. This could be a day at a spa, a weekend yoga retreat, or a trip to someplace you've always wanted to go.

Aunt Ida Tweaks It

I think this is a great idea! As I said before, start from where you are. The only person who can make your life worth living is you.

Number-One Priority

I learned about marriage from my parents. They were married just shy of fifty years, and they had the kind of good, strong marriage that time and commitment bring. As Dad says, "A good marriage is like a good fire; you have to tend it to make it burn bright."

> *"A good marriage is like a good fire; you have to tend it to make it burn bright."*

Growing up, our parents used to tell Irene and me, "Our number-one priority is to each other, you girls second. 'Cause if we don't take care of our marriage, we won't have a foundation strong enough to support this family."

That may sound shocking nowadays where all the focus seems to be on putting children first. But as a kid, I found this notion very comforting. First off, our parents told us outright what they were doing. Kids love to know what's going on. Second, our parents never felt guilty for spending time together without us girls. They didn't believe they were doing anything wrong, so Irene and me didn't either. And third, they were always so happy when they got back from a breakfast out or an overnight in Bangor. Plus, we still did a lot of stuff together as a family. Except for their dates, they took us most everywhere with them. But spending time with Irene and me never seemed like an obligation to our parents. They were energized in their relationship, and they shared that energy and enthusiasm for life with us.

Looking back, I realize that my parents didn't have a lot of extra money, but they always managed to scrape together a little for a date. Sometimes I think they just bought a couple of beers at Blue's general store, drove up to the Moose Megantic Lake overlook, otherwise known as Makeout Point, parked, and talked (or whatever). Making their marriage a priority wasn't about spending money; it was about spending time together, just the two of them.

Sex. That's Right. I Said Sex.

Now that I got your attention, all I'm saying on that subject is, "Yes."

Sex is important in a relationship, sure. But affection is the key. That's what I miss most if Charlie's away for a long week-end Ski-Dooing. I miss holding hands. I miss kissing.

Charlie and me always kiss each other good-bye and hello. It worked for my parents, and it works for us. If I'm getting dressed in the morning and Charlie's ready to leave for work, he'll come into the bedroom and kiss me good-bye. When he gets home from work, I stop what I'm doing (usually fixing supper) and kiss him hello.

Think about it. Which is more appealing: yelling "Good-bye!" as you're going out the door and your spouse yelling back, "Have a nice day!" from the other room, or having this tiny moment of connection when you're coming and going. It says, "You're important to me." Just a quick kiss. This seems like such a little thing, but it's huge!

Mysterious Injuries

"Tending a fire is a delicate thing," my dad says. "If you leave it be too long, it'll go out. But if you put too much wood on it, you'll smother the flame."

Once again, there has to be a balance. Making quality time with your husband a priority is a good thing. Being with him every waking moment of the day, not so much. It's important to have things you do together and things you do with your friends or by yourself. Spending time with the Women Who Run with the Moose makes me happy, and I bring that joy back to the relationship.

117

It's the same with Charlie and the boys. Though sometimes what Charlie brings back is not joy, but mysterious injuries. That's because these guys are at the age where their bodies are just not capable of doing what they used to do, but their minds haven't caught on to this fact. And when Charlie comes back home, hobbling, I, being the good wife that I am, try to muster up a little sympathy, but it's hard, considering the circumstances.

Last spring, Charlie and the boys, Bud, Smitty, Pat, Tommy, and Junior (aka, the husbands of the Women Who Run with the Moose) went up to an old fishing camp that's been in Smitty's family for generations. I can't tell you where it is, 'cause the boys took a "blood oath" never to reveal its location, even (or especially) to their wives. So, you get the mentality we're dealing with here. Goes without saying, there's no cell-phone coverage. Who knows if that's really true, but that's their story and they're sticking to it.

> *When the boys get together for this sort of outing, they get what we call "duffer brain." You know how bees and ants are of one mind, all linked together so they can get things done? Well, the boys get like that, too. I'm guessing testosterone's got something to do with it. That and Pabst Blue Ribbon.*

The boys left late Friday and returned Sunday afternoon with no fish, only injuries. Charlie's back was all screwed up, Tommy had cut his hand, Bud broke his ankle, and Junior's truck was missing part of its muffler. Other than that, they had a great time!

Us girls tried to piece together the story, but it's sketchy. That's because when the boys get together for this sort of outing, they get what we call "duffer brain." You know how bees and ants are of one mind, all linked together so they can get things done? Well, the boys get like that, too. I'm guessing testosterone's got something to do with it. That, and Pabst Blue Ribbon. They're linked together, all right, but their decision-making leaves a little something to be desired.

"Charlie," I says, "you're home early. You have a good time?"

"It was different."

Then I notice he's walking funny. "Is your back out?"

"Yeah, I pulled it carrying Bud to the truck."

"Oh my God, is he all right?"

"A broken ankle is all."

"What happened?"

"Oh, he got up to take a leak in the night and fell off the porch."

"Yikes! Didn't he bring a flashlight out with him?"

"Batteries burned out."

"I thought you brought extra batteries with you."

"Too muddy to get the truck up the road. Bottomed out halfway up. We got it unstuck, but the muffler broke off. Decided to leave the truck there and haul in the supplies by foot. It was a couple of miles, so we only brought the essentials."

"Batteries seem pretty essential to me."

"Smitty thought he had some up to camp. Anyways, we had to haul in the cooler and the fishing stuff. Could only carry so much."

"So," I says, joking around, "you took the beer and left behind the water and the first-aid kit, right?"

There was a pregnant pause.

"You left behind the water and the first-aid kit?" I repeated.

"I told you, we could only carry so much. Had to make hard decisions."

> *Tommy sliced his hand the first morning using a knife to open a bag of fried pork rinds or something. They sterilized it with some whiskey and cut up a T-shirt to use as a bandage.*
>
> *"Sweetheart," I says, "you don't get bonus points for solving a problem that arises from sheer stupidity."*

And it just went downhill from there. Tommy sliced his hand the first morning using a knife to open a bag of fried pork rinds or something. They sterilized it with some whiskey and cut up a T-shirt to use as a bandage. Charlie seemed proud of this ingenuity.

"Sweetheart," I says, "you don't get bonus points for solving a problem that arises from sheer stupidity."

"It wasn't that big a cut. Just ten stitches."

"Excuse me?"

"When we brought Bud to the emergency room, they sewed up Tommy's hand. No big deal. It was starting to get infected, so they gave him some antibiotics. And a tetanus shot."

Charlie said that while Bud was getting an X-ray, he and the boys started talking about how they're getting older and might need to make some changes in how they do things. Then duffer brain kicked in with a great idea. "Let's open up the group to a new member. How about a hot-looking nurse who likes to cook, hunt, fish, and Ski-Doo?!"

In your dreams, boys!

 Straight Talk from the Barcalounger: A Happy Wife Makes for a Happy Husband

The key to a happy marriage? Look interested and say, "Yes, dear."

You think I'm joking, but it's true!

And tell her she looks nice. Took me a while to catch on to that one. Sure, if we were going out on the town and she was all dolled up, I'd say something. But that's not enough.

Bottom line: Whether the two of you are going to a bean supper, or she's off for a girls' night out, or if she's just going to work, your wife's put some effort into how she looks. Even if you feel she's missed the mark, compliment her. Say something like, "Don't you look sharp tonight, deah," or "Aren't you something?" You're not being dishonest. You're showing her you notice and appreciate her. It's about rewarding effort, not outcome. Trust me, just doing this one thing will improve the quality of your married life no end, 'cause a happy wife makes for a happy husband.

The "Honey Do" List

There's no doubt about it—men and women are just built different. So I'm not into this "let's share all the housework" stuff. We tried that once when we first got married, and it was awful. (This is when the women's lib stuff was getting going.) We set aside a Saturday morning and divided up the chores: I dusted the house and cleaned the bathroom, Charlie vacuumed and tidied up the kitchen. That was the theory anyways. What we ended up with was a poorly cleaned house and lots of bad attitude. Not just from Charlie 'cause he didn't want to be doing housework, but from me, too, thinking he wasn't doing the job good enough.

That was it. From then on we moved to a separate, but equal approach to chores. Like moose, we each have our own territory. For the most part, I take care of the inside of the house: cleaning, grocery shopping, and cooking. Charlie takes care of the outside: snow blowing and mowing the lawn. There's a little crossover. We do the dishes and pay bills together. Charlie takes

> *Actually, I think Charlie's better with a list of chores he can cross off. (Trouble comes when he starts improvising.)*

care of any repairs or emergencies (plugged toilet, leaky faucet). I plant the annuals, tend to the potted plants, and do a little weeding from time to time. But by and large, the house is my department and the yard is Charlie's. He's got one of them zero-turn mowers that he just loves. Has a shed with a ramp he keeps it in.

Oh, and I come up with the punch list of bigger things that need to be done: Charlie's "Honey Do" list. I'm very good at that; I guess you could say it's my specialty. And he doesn't complain, God bless him. Actually, I think Charlie's better with a list of chores he can cross off. (Trouble comes when he starts improvising.) But so long as he sticks to my list, he's great. And Charlie's always so proud of what he's accomplished.

"Ida, I moved that little lilac like you wanted."

Even if I'm in the middle of doing something, I go outside and do some appreciating. That's perhaps the most important part of any "Honey Do" list, and don't you forget it. Your task as the maker of the list is to tell him what a great job he did, how nice it looks. Oh, and don't forget to say thank you. Throw in one of his favorite meals, and you're golden the next time you ask him to do something around the house.

Now, this is not an automatic vice-versa kind of thing, unfortunately. After a day of vigorous housecleaning, your husband is not going to come home and start admiring all your handiwork. It just ain't gonna happen. It's not that he doesn't care; it's that he doesn't notice. You could be at it all day, dusting, vacuuming, cleaning the bathroom, and washing knickknacks, curtains, and rugs. You may have even cleaned out a bookcase or some shelves.

How about the linen closet and the catch-all drawer, now all nice and neat? He'll walk in and go, "What's for supper?"

Don't waste time and energy getting mad at him. It's just a fact of life. The thing is, you have to tell him what you've done, and in some cases, show him. "Honey, come see the catch-all drawer!"

Once you point out all the hard work you've been doing, if he's worth his weight in salt, he'll go, "Thank you," or "That looks great, honey!" Which is your opening to say, "I thought we'd go out to dinner tonight. How about a DQ burger and some onion rings? Maybe split a brownie sundae for dessert?"

Needless to say, that kind of evening is a lot more fun than the alternative. You know what I'm talking about. After a day of housecleaning, you spend the evening banging and slamming things in the kitchen as you get dinner ready. Or moping around the house, staring forlornly into space, sighing, giving him the silent treatment.

Take pity on him, and yourself. In a world where so many things are out of our control, this, for heaven's sake, is doable. Take time to appreciate your husband, and point him in the right direction so he can appreciate you.

Charlie Gets a Massage

Marriage doesn't mean you have to do everything together. Don't get me wrong. I love hanging out with Charlie, but I also enjoy my own company. Besides, there are some things you just know are going to be a stretch for your spouse, and are just going be a lot more fun with your friends. Or by yourself.

Like last May, Charlie and me went for a massage. Yes, you read that right. Charlie got a massage, and not by me. By a guy named Michael.

See, for Christmas, our niece Caitlin gave us each a gift certificate for a one hour massage. She knows how much I love being pampered, but frankly, I think Charlie would have been just as happy with one of them Hickory Farms cheese logs, you know, the ones with the little nuts on the outside?

God love her, Caitlin's heart is in the right place. She knew how stressful it had been for Charlie at work, what with all the layoffs down to the mill. Plus, winter means extra wear and tear on my hubby what with all the snow blowing, roof raking, and shoveling.

Besides, Caitlin said her boyfriend Adam loves getting a massage. Though somehow, I think Caitlin's the one giving the massage, and it ends with more than just a glass of water and a tip!

When he unwrapped his gift, Charlie pretended to be happy, "Wow! Would you look at that? Isn't that something?"

Afterwards, he says, "Here."

"What are you doing?"

"I'm giving you my gift certificate. You love getting a massage."

"That I do. And I'd like to oblige you, Charlie, but no go."

"Why not?"

"Because that was a thoughtful gift from Caitlin. And she'll know you didn't use it because she'll ask. I don't want to hurt her feelings and neither do you."

"Oh, I guess not."

So I made our appointment. And had to reschedule. Twice. But we finally went last May. I said it was part of my birthday celebration. Charlie couldn't argue with that.

I'd scheduled our appointments for the same time, but in separate rooms. I just don't get that couples massage thing. I want to be off in my own little world. I chose a guy masseuse for Charlie, figuring he'd relax more. You know, he wouldn't be worried about getting overly stimulated, if you catch my drift.

Oh, I was wicked excited about it, but you'd think Charlie was going to a firing squad. I says to him, "You looking forward to your massage?"

"Nope. Got yard work to do."

"Oh, for God's sake, Charlie! Suck it up! It's a massage, not an execution!"

"I leave on my underwear, right?"

"You can if you want. I don't."

"I'm not getting naked with some guy."

"Suit yourself."

To be honest, Charlie looked kind of funny sitting there in the inner waiting area, filling out the paperwork. It's all dim lights and new agey music. Some guy's chanting away, another's banging a gong. Charlie looks over at me like, What the hell?

Then this big fella dressed in what looks like turquoise pajamas come into the waiting room, "Charlie?"

"Yup."

"I'm Michael. Come with me."

Charlie casts a worried look at me as he disappears down the hall.

Afterwards, I says to him, "So, how was it?"

"Michael gave me a chocolate."

"Don't worry. Doesn't mean you're dating. Christine gave me one, too. Did you find it at all relaxing?"

"Every once in a while, it hurt like a bastard."

"That's how you can tell it's a good massage. They're really working the kinks out."

"Okay, but I still don't see the appeal."

> *And I know that every morning he's going to have half a banana on his cereal. Don't matter if it's a big banana or a small one, just half a banana 'cause that's how Charlie rolls.*

"I'm proud of you, Charlie, for soldiering on. Why don't we stop in at the Busy Bee on the way home, and get some lunch? My treat."

That brightened his mood. "Sounds good. Want my chocolate?"

That's my guy!

When you've been married as long was we have, there are some things you just know. Like I knew getting a massage would be a stretch for Charlie. I know he's never going to get the entire concept of "guest towels." And I know that every morning he's going to have half a banana on his cereal. Don't matter if it's a big banana or a small one, just half a banana 'cause that's how Charlie rolls.

She Was a Nice-Looking Gal, and I Like Pickles

When it comes to having a happy marriage, a sense of humor is right up there with respect. I've heard people say this about work, but I think it applies to relationships, too. Take your marriage seriously, but not yourself.

I was reminded of this when I was walking Scamp one Saturday morning, and I run into Hank and Pearl Plaistead. They were just getting back from breakfast down to the Busy Bee.

"We go early to get a good seat," Pearl says. "Hank just loves to watch folks from away plunk down $4.50 for a cup of coffee."

"Ah," I reply, "Babe's special Maine Mocha Latte Grandé!"

"Better known as Maxwell House poured over a Hershey's Kiss, topped with Cool Whip."

Hank pipes up, "Hey, if folks want to pay through the nose for some fancy-schmancy coffee, Babe's only willing to oblige."

"Gee," I says, "we sure have had a lot of tourists this summer, huh? Gotta leave ten minutes early to get to work, what with all the traffic."

"Yup," Hank replies. "Get this: I was working here in the yard a few weeks back, and this fella from Massachusetts pulls up sharp in front of the house. Doesn't say 'hi,' or nothing. Just jumps right in. 'Who owns that land back there?' he asks. 'Do you own that land back there?'

"I says, 'No, I don't own that land back there.'

" 'Well, who owns that land back there?'

"And I says, 'God owns that land back there. I'm just maintaining it for Him.' "

"Aren't you a smart aleck, Hank."

"Ida," Pearl chimes in, "you don't know the half of it."

I go, "You know, I don't think I've ever asked how you two met."

Pearl doesn't miss a beat. "Over a plate of pickles at my aunt's house. It was Thanksgiving, and I'm bringing a plate of pickles into the dining room. I come 'round the corner and there's Hank, standing in the doorway to the living room. He smiles at me, and that was it."

"Wow!" I says. "Love at first sight!"

"Well," Hank chimes in, "she was a nice-looking gal, and I like pickles."

Pearl continues. "Later that week, my aunt calls up and invites me to dinner Saturday night. Guess who else is there?"

"Aren't you the fast worker, Hank?"

Hank winks. "Yeah, I was pretty wild back then. Pearl fell in love with me right quick, and you know what? She's been falling out of love with me ever since!"

"I find that hard to believe."

"I'm telling you, Ida—Pearl's been cleaning up a storm lately, getting rid of old stuff. I'm afraid I'm next."

"Hank, you are so full of it," Pearl replies. "I'm gonna have to go get my hip waders. The manure's piling up fast!"

"You two lovebirds got anything special planned this week-end?"

"Hank and me are going to our daughter Sally's place over to Veazie. She's throwing us a little anniversary dinner."

Hank goes, "Thirty-five happy years together."

"Wait a minute," I says. "I thought you celebrated your fifti-eth a while back."

"We did."

"Don't listen to him, Ida. It's more like twenty-five good years, anyway!"

Coping with Loss

Now, Charlie and me are at that age where some of our friends have lost a wife or a husband. It's a reminder to appreci-ate the time you have together, because even the best marriage doesn't last forever.

I was reminded of this a while back, when I went down to the Wally Mart with my friend Celina. Since her husband, Henry, died, we try to get together once a month or so and do something. Celina was looking for a new lipstick, and I was act-ing as her beauty consultant—you know, providing moral sup-port. Plus, I'm always up for a little browsing.

Charlie and me had kind of a special bond with Celina and Henry, who, like us, never had children. We did a lot of things together as couples, especially in our twenties and thirties when most folks our age were busy with their kids.

But they were a little older than us, and when Henry took early retirement from Central Maine Power, they became snowbirds, spending half their time in Florida.

It broke my heart when Henry got sick. I can't stand to see people suffer. He was a fighter, though. When he became house-bound, I'd go visit once a week, bring a little treat for him to eat, free Celina up to go run an errand or two. I never heard Henry complain all the times I visited, even that last time, when I brought him some of my special vanilla pudding.

Forty-five years, that's how long they were married. And they still acted like newlyweds. Henry called her his "bride," and Celina referred to him as "my Henry," as in "My Henry did this," and "My Henry said that." It would have been obnoxious if they weren't so cute.

> *At the wake, Celina says to me, "Ida, I still have the dress I wore to our thirtieth anniversary party. My Henry loved me in that dress. That's what I want to be buried in, so I look pretty when my Henry sees me in heaven. Promise me you'll make sure they bury me in that dress. I've gained a little weight, so just slice it up the back."*

At the wake, Celina says to me, "Ida, I still have the dress I wore to our thirtieth anniversary party. My Henry loved me in that dress. That's what I want to be buried in, so I look pretty when my Henry sees me in heaven. Promise me you'll make sure they bury me in that dress. I've gained a little weight, so just slice it up the back."

Spending time with Celina, seeing her without her Henry, always makes me hug Charlie a little tighter. Sure, he may get on my nerves from time to time, but truth is, I just can't picture my life without him.

Four years on, Celina's bounced back better than I'd've thought. We grow 'em tough up here in the North Country. She's still got a tinge of sadness around her eyes, but she's joined the Senior Center and attends their monthly meetings. She's even gone on a few day trips with 'em, including down to the big flower show in Portland, and to the Maine State Music Theater to see *My Fair Lady*.

So, after our successful outing at the Wally Mart (I found a nice pink nail polish, and Celina got a lipstick in the prettiest shade of coral that looks adorable on her!), we went down to the DQ to celebrate. Over Peanut Buster Parfaits, Celina confided, "Ida, last night, I had a revelation. Made me feel a little guilty."

"Really, Celina? Do tell!"

"Well, you know how much I miss my Henry, right?"

"Goes without saying."

"Okay. So last night I'm standing in the bathroom, checking my eyebrows for stray hairs, putting on my night cream, flossing my teeth, when I hear a strange noise. Turns out, it's me, humming. I look at myself in the mirror, and I'm smiling. And at that moment, I realize: I miss my Henry in every room of this house, except here."

"In the bathroom?"

"Yup! Ida, I confess. I just love having a sink to myself."

"The stuff of dreams, Celina. It's the stuff of dreams!"

It's different for men, of course. After our mother died, Dad seemed kind of lost. Irene and me looked after him, but we couldn't be with him every minute of the day. Besides, he needed room to grieve. Eventually, Dad figured out little

> *He'd buy his groceries one day at a time, so's he'd have a reason to get dressed and get out of the house.*

ways to cope. The hardest time for him was in the evening, so he adjusted his schedule. Instead of reading the newspaper first thing in the morning, he started reading it after supper. He'd buy his groceries one day at a time, so's he'd have a reason to get dressed and get out of the house. Irene and me would bring him meals or have him over to dinner a couple times a week, and we helped him find a cleaning person.

But in the end, Dad found the house was too much for him, so a few years after our mom passed, he sold it and moved into Mahoosuc Green, which is one of them senior living facilities. He has the cutest little apartment. Irene and me helped him fix it up. Let me tell you, Dad is having the time of his life. He looks about ten years younger than when our mother was sick. He's always

off bowling or golfing or on bus trips to Foxwoods or Quebec City. He barely has time to get a haircut. And those widows are buzzing around him like flies to honey—he's a good catch, a nice-looking man, good head of hair, and he can still drive

> *And those widows are buzzing around him like flies to honey—he's a good catch, a nice-looking man, good head of hair, and he can still drive at night.*

at night. I told him, "Dad, you're in a seller's market. You play your cards right, you could have a different casserole every night of the week, if you know what I'm saying."

Togetherness in Mahoosuc Mills Is . . .

- Frank and Ada Jones. They've been married seventy-five years. Frank is as deaf as a post. Says he got that way out of self-defense 'cause Ada could talk the ears off a dead donkey. "Well," Ada says, looking at him and smiling, "now I know why my eyesight is shot."
- Whitey Hebert and his son Little Whitey. They say they're in the junktique business, but mostly they just ride around looking for free stuff. If they put as much effort into working as they do into avoiding work, they'd be millionaires.
- Earl Brown and his pet billy goat, Fred. You think I'm making this up, but I'm not. Earl goes everywhere with that goat. Fred wears a straw hat in summer and a knit cap in winter, is housebroken, and quite a good companion, to hear Earl tell it. Just don't stand downwind of 'em.
- The three-legged race at the Blackfly Festival. Warning: should not be attempted after age fifty.

A Wedding Toast

Last August, my goddaughter, Hilary, married Rick, the love of her life. Charlie and me were there when they took the plunge—literally. They exchanged vows in their bathing suits, then held hands and jumped into Hallowell Pond. I believe everyone has the perfect marriage ceremony for them, and Hilary and Rick's celebration suited them to a T.

Their reception was held at the Dugall Farm, complete with wildflowers on the picnic tables and a pig roasting over an open spit. Before the dancing got started, I did a little toast to the happy couple. I thought I'd share it with you here:

"Wives, there may come a time when your husband is getting on your nerves. I mean, he's breathing too loud. I know this sounds what they call 'counterintuitive,' but when Charlie's irritating the hell out of me, I bake him a batch of his favorite cookies. Really! Doing something nice for him usually turns my mood around. And if it doesn't, I take a bunch of them cookies into my craft room and shut the door.

"That said, husbands, if your wife makes you some of your favorite cookies, you know you're in trouble. It took Charlie about twenty years to figure this out, and I want to save you the pain.

"If your wife is moping around the house and you can't figure out what's wrong, asking her what's wrong is not going to help you, because she's just going to say 'nothing' and sink deeper into despair because you can't read her mind. So if your wife is moping around, most likely it's because of something you did or did not do. Or the cumulative effect of the many things you did or did not do. It don't matter what, you don't have to know. Just go up to her, look her in the eye, and say, 'Sweetheart, I'm sorry.' Then wrap your arms around her and give her a hug. I mean, a big bear hug, and say, 'I love you.'

"Now, this is the pivotal moment. Here's where a lot of men mess up. I can't stress this enough. Do not, I repeat, do not break that hug too soon. If you do, all your hard work will go down the drain. How soon is too soon? Well, you can't go wrong if you just keep hugging. Rub her back. Let her cry into your shoulder. Wait until your wife breaks the hug. Then give her a kiss or two or three. Before you know it, you'll be eating cookies together."

Gettin' Going

- Say please and thank you to your spouse. You don't have to make a big deal about it. Just do it.
- Plan a regular date night with your husband. Put it on the calendar.
- Kiss your spouse hello and good-bye for a week. Hold hands when you get the chance.
- Ask your husband to do something around the house. The more specific, the better; that way he'll stay on task. Then when he's done, take time to appreciate it.
- The next time you do something around the house, tell your husband. Do not wait for him to notice on his own.
- Do something nice for your husband if he is driving you crazy, like bake cookies or cook his favorite dinner. Don't do something that involves him 'cause that'll just make things worse. It's just you, by your lonesome, trying to change your mood by doing a good deed.
- Give up the notion that your husband can read your mind. He can't, and he never, ever will.

Seven

A Moose Does
What a Moose Does Best

A moose doesn't have to work, of course, unless you count foraging for food and procreating. (Seriously, how can I get a job like that, right?) A moose does what a moose does best.

For the rest of us, finding what we do best, or at least finding a job that we can tolerate, isn't always easy. And frankly, sometimes work seems to get in the way of having fun, doesn't it?

However, work is a fact of life, for most of us anyways. So, you have two choices: be miserable for forty hours a week, or not. Now, you don't have to love every minute you spend at work. That's not realistic. But at the very least, we're shooting for neutral. In neutral, you can coast as opposed to being resentful at work, which can jam up the gears and make for a bumpy ride. And your resentment won't end at work because resentment is the kind of thing that spills over into the rest of your life.

At the same time, the benefits of working can spill over too: getting out of the house, interacting with folks you wouldn't normally see, getting satisfaction from a job well done. A good day at work can energize you and give you confidence. And, of course, you bring those feelings home with you.

A Little Flirting Never Hurts

One Friday afternoon a while back, I'm standing at my register down to the A&P, staring into space, when a nice-looking fella from away steps up and asks me where the canned beans are.

"Aisle three," I tell him. "Right-hand side, quarter of the way down."

"Thank you, miss," he says, smiling. Then, I swear, he winks at me. Winks! It took me by surprise, so I giggled. Couldn't believe it! It just popped out.

So, he finds his beans and a few other essentials, a couple boxes of macaroni and cheese and a six-pack of Bud, and comes to me to cash out even though two other registers were open. Says he's from down around Augusta, here to do a little hunting.

I'm trying to be helpful, you know, an ambassador for Mahoosuc Mills, so I says, "If you're hankering for some home cooking, there's a baked bean supper down to the Congo Church tomorrow night. Five o'clock."

"I might be up for that," he says. "Are you going to be there?"

"Oh, yes," I tell him. "The Congo Church has one of the best bean suppers around. I wouldn't miss it."

He flashes that smile again. "Maybe I'll see you there."

"Maybe you will."

He winks again and strolls out the door. I can't remember the last time some fella flirted with me. Darned if it didn't put a spring in my step.

That night, I cooked two of Charlie's favorites—meat loaf and apple pie. And we had ourselves a romantic evening together—once I convinced him to shut off the tube and come to bed.

Finding a Better Job

This is where I'm supposed to talk about leaving your job as a receptionist and turning your design for the perfect paper clip into a multimillion-dollar corporation.

Well, not exactly, but I do see articles like that all the time. I find them inspiring, but a little depressing—kind of like that "half their size" issue of *People* magazine. I don't have any brilliant business ideas, and even if I did, I'm not interested in running my own company.

I do think that a big part of livin' the good life is doing work that's right for you—that plays to your strengths. But how do you find that work, right? You can start by asking yourself, "What do I love to do?" Now, it's real easy to get bogged down when asking that kind of question because you start thinking about specific jobs like gardener or movie critic or cookbook author, which narrows the field right off quick and eliminates a lot of jobs that you might like. Plus, it can seem like such a big leap from where you are to where you want to be that you end up closed for business before you even start.

I believe asking yourself more general questions will help you come up with possible jobs that are a good fit for you. Here are some examples to help get you headed in the right direction:

- How much security do I need?
- Do I want to work for the town, a business, or for myself?
- Do I want flexible hours or a set schedule?
- Do I like interacting with people or being by myself?
- High heels or comfortable shoes?
- Dress up or dress down?
- Do I need to be surrounded by beautiful things or good smells?

- Do I want every day to be different or do I like a routine?
- Indoors or outdoors?
- Do I like sleeping late or am I an early-morning person?
- How do I like to work? For example, some people like a job with strict guidelines and a due date. Others like seeing what needs to be done and doing it without being asked. Then there are the people in between who want to be given a job and a due date, but be left alone to do it. Which are you?

To help find out, ask yourself important questions like:
- What's the best job I ever had?
- Why'd I like it?
- What parts of the job I have now am I not so crazy about?
- What parts do I like?

That last one was really important for my sister, Irene. She'd been working at Mahoosuc Savings Bank for years and liked it okay, but felt she needed a change after our mother died.

"What do you like most about the bank?" I ask her.

"Well," she says, "I like it when someone like Frances Mitchell comes in, and she's in a mess with her checking account 'cause Harold took care of all the finances. Then he up and died and left her clueless. So Frances comes into the bank and I help straighten things out and teach her how to use a checkbook. I guess that's what I like best."

"Do you like doing that with just older people, or all ages?"

"You know, I think I really like working with older folks, helping 'em out."

"Well, you were great with Mom when she was sick."

So now, Irene works down to the Senior Center. Sure, it pays a little less, but money isn't everything. Irene helps folks with all sorts of things: organizes drivers to take 'em to appointments, plans activities, and does her fair share of light bookkeeping. And, it turns out, Irene really loves that every day is a little different, as opposed to the bank where it was pretty much the same routine. She wasn't miserable at the bank, you understand, but now she's genuinely happy. And that happiness and the energy it brings ripples over into the rest of her life, and things seem more balanced.

Work in Mahoosuc Mills Is . . .

* Not as plentiful as it used to be, so thank God us Maineiacs are stubborn and resourceful.
* At any public event, trying to carry on a conversation with, well, let's keep them nameless. Charlie and me call 'em the "Hard-to-Talk-to Gang." You must know folks like that, too.
* Staying for the whole Town Meeting. My hats off to anyone who can tough it out to the end, 'cause I don't have the patience for it.

 Straight Talk from the Barcalounger: A Job Is a Job Is a Job
    Your job is something you do so you can afford to do the things you like to do: take a vacation, buy your toys (like snowmobiles), and put food on the table. End of story.

Women are always talking about balancing work and home life. I think it's men who have a problem with this. For those of you who put all of your eggs in the work-basket, I say get a life! Yeah, yeah, you're working so hard for your family at home, but if that's all you do, you won't have a family to come home to. Trust me, I've seen it happen.

I'm a foreman down to the mill. Worked there since I graduated high school. It's been rough the last few years with the layoffs and all, but I'm lucky to have a job, in my opinion. So I show up, do my best, then go home to Ida and Scamp, and that makes it all worthwhile. 'Cause in the end, a job is a job is a job.

You Got to Be Here, So Be Here

When it comes to work (and life), I think it's important to have your own personal definition of success. What does *success* mean to you? Is it about prestige or being happy? Is it about punching the clock, putting in time and getting the heck out of there, or taking pride in your work?

I don't know about you, but it bugs the hell out of me to walk up to the checkout in a store and hear the person behind the register say, "Did you find everything you were looking for?" or "Have a nice day," delivered in a monotone with no eye contact. I'm thinking, You got to be here, so be here. It's a lot more fun if you actually talk to customers and connect with them. And for God's sake, take that gum out of your mouth!

I just don't get it. I love being a cashier down to the A&P. Now, it may not seem like the most prestigious job to some, but it's the perfect job for me. I enjoy knowing what's going on in town. I like the security, and I like having seniority, good benefits, and a great schedule—Monday through Friday—eleven to five. It's important to me that I don't take my job home with me. When I'm at work, I do my best, and when I punch out, that's it.

It hasn't all been smooth sailing, though. We hit a rough patch a few years back, but eventually things settled back down to normal, thank goodness.

See, it all started three, maybe four winters ago, when good old Fred Nichols, who had owned the store since I can remember, passed away in the produce section, poor fella. The place was inherited by his kids. They both live away and had no interest whatsoever in coming back to Mahoosuc Mills to run the store. So, what do they do? They sell out to that big chain, Super Food World (though, as I said earlier, everyone in town still calls it the A&P).

> *I says to him, "Listen, I've known most of these folks my whole life. I know what to say to them." Us employees started calling it "Stupid Food World."*

Our new boss was a kid who didn't even look old enough to vote. William Davenport III, or "Chip," as he asked us to call him, had never run a grocery store, but apparently learned all about it in college. First thing he does? Puts all these new rules and regulations in place, like what we're supposed to say to customers. I says to him, "Listen, I've known most of these folks my whole life. I know what to say to them." Us employees started calling it "Stupid Food World."

Poor Chip. I don't know how he survived that first year. I asked him about it later, and he said if he could survive the hazing he took to get into his college fraternity—he told me the name of the fraternity, but I can't remember; it's all Greek to me—he could take what we dished out. It probably helped that his girlfriend, Tiffany, moved to Mahoosuc Mills with him.

Tiffany was this skinny little thing, blonde, dressed all trendy, but alas, none too lively in the brains department. We called her "Dip"—Get it? Chip and Dip?

Tiffany didn't last too long in Mahoosuc Mills. One winter did her in, and she hightailed it back down to Portland. Now Chip's dating Tom and Brenda Bragdon's girl, Cindy. They make a cute couple, and she's rubbed off on him. He's more flexible now, and isn't afraid to roll up his sleeves if something needs to be done.

Iceberg, Romaine, or Red Leaf?
Step In and Help When You Can

Hands down, my favorite part of working at the A&P is talking with people and helping 'em out.

Like a while back, I'm standing at my station, Register 3, when who do I see in the produce section but James Brown. No, not James Brown, the Godfather of Soul, the hardest-working man in show business, who is now singing duets with Elvis in that great showroom in the sky. I'm talking about James Brown, CPA, father of three, and the hardest-working accountant in Mahoosuc Mills. Well, truth be told, he's the only accountant in Mahoosuc Mills now that his father has retired. James may be sharp with numbers, but there he was, hovering over the lettuce, looking perplexed.

James married a gal he met at Dartmouth, Courtney Van Buren. The two of 'em worked in Boston until they were ready to start a family, then they moved back to Mahoosuc Mills to raise the kids. Courtney elected not to change her name, so all the kids are hyphenated Van Buren-Brown. Seems kind of cumbersome to me, but to each his own. Courtney telecommutes to some software development–type job in Portland. I know that means she works from home, but I hear the word telecommute, and all I can think of is *Harry Potter*, when they travel by chimney. You know, they step into the chimney and go up in a puff of smoke. Then, pop! They materialize in another chimney someplace else. I picture Courtney disappearing down the phone line and reappearing with a bang and a puff of smoke somewhere in Portland.

> *I know that means she works from home, but I hear the word telecommute, and all I can think of is Harry Potter, when they travel by chimney.*

Because James works in town, Courtney occasionally has him pick up some groceries on his way home. Oh, it's just pitiful to watch. James doesn't have the temperament for it. "There are too many variables," he told me once.

So anyway, there's James, list in hand, beads of sweat on his forehead, pacing back and forth in front of the lettuce: iceberg, romaine, red leaf, green leaf, spring mix, herb mix, and hydroponic. (Not bad for our little A&P, huh?)

Get anything but iceberg, I'm thinking. I got nothing against iceberg myself, but I know Courtney does. The only time I've seen her buy it was when she was having a "retro party," as she called it.

"That sounds interesting," I says to her. "What are you serving?"

"For appetizers, pigs in a blanket and celery stuffed with cream cheese, followed by pork chops cooked in cream of mushroom soup—have you ever heard of such a thing?—scalloped potatoes and big wedges of iceberg lettuce smothered in Russian dressing. And for dessert—are you ready?—Twinkies, Suzy Q's, and Ring Dings."

I'm thinking, throw in some ambrosia salad and it sounds like the menu for the LeClair family reunion.

James sighs, takes out his cell phone, and calls Courtney.

Remember when grocery shopping was easy? I mean, I sympathize with James. Used to be iceberg was your only choice. You'd pick up the first one that still had a little life in it.

After a quick conversation, James puts the phone back in his pocket, grabs the red leaf, looks back at his list, and moves on.

The front door opens. I see Chip pushing a line of grocery carts into the store. What a beautiful sight. It took us forever to break him in, but it was worth the effort.

"Hey, Ida, how you doing?"

"Oh fine, Chip. Just another quiet day here in scenic Mahoosuc Mills."

Chip pushes the grocery carts into their place at the front of the store. "Ida, I'll be in the office if anyone needs me.

"Sure thing, Chip."

I glance back at the produce section and there's James staring at the apples. Good luck, dear, I think. He sighs and takes out the cell phone again. Pink Ladies are my personal favorite. Then, in this order, Crispin Pink, Braeburn, and Fuji. Except if I'm using the apples for cooking, then I like Macintosh or Granny Smith.

James puts the phone back in his pocket and continues to stare at the apples. He looks pleadingly in my direction. "Cortland?" he asks.

"End of the aisle, to your left. They're on special this week."

"Thanks, Ida," he says, tearing off one of them plastic bags from the roll and struggling to get the top open.

I finish ringing out Nancy Landry and turn back to the produce section. James is still there, still looking lost. I switch off my Register 3 light and walk over to him.

"Help," he says, handing me the list.

"Let's see. What do we have here? Parsley. I believe Courtney prefers curly leaf. There, James, to your right. And what's this? 3 V.R. tom. Hmmm. That must be vine ripe tomatoes. On the stand over there. And fennel. Oh dear, we're out of fennel. Won't have it until tomorrow."

He looks at me, stricken.

"Don't panic, James! We're just going to have to bring in the heavy artillery."

I take him by the hand and walk him over to the flower section. "I'm thinking these yellow tulips'll do the trick."

James smiles and stands up straighter. "Ida, you're a lifesaver."

"Thanks, dear. Now, if you're up for it, grab a bottle of her favorite wine and one of them big Lindt bars—I highly recommend the milk chocolate crème brûlée—and neither one of you will miss the fennel!"

Just then Chip walks by, smiles, and winks at me.

Now that was a good day at work!

What Happens at Smitty's, Stays at Smitty's

As I said earlier, one of the things I like about my job is that when I'm there, I'm there, but when I'm not, I'm not. Most of the time, anyways.

Leaving work behind at the end of the day is easier said than done for a lot of folks. That's a wicked drain of your energy, and if you don't find a way to deal with it, it can interfere with your home life, too.

Take my dear friend Rita. She's one of the sweetest gals I know. Nice as can be. Too nice, if you know what I'm saying. She works down to Smitty's Hardware with her husband, Smitty. She's worked there since she married him, and she knows her stuff inside out. Watching her in action brings me up short. See,

Rita is this little wisp of a thing and always all dolled up. She doesn't look like she could even put gas in her car.

Anyways, I'll stop by Smitty's to say hi, and I might find Cy Thibodeau asking Rita for advice on how to rewire his house. And I'll see Rita going on about circuits, volts, and running cables, and I don't know what all. Rita just loves helping folks find items they're looking for and givin' them advice.

Unfortunately, some folks want more than a little advice. They want you to tell 'em how to do their plumbing project, soup to nuts. "And maybe you could drop by on your way home, just to make sure I'm doing it right," one of the customers might say to Rita. "I got arthritis in my elbow and can't really tighten stuff up all the way."

Me? I'd tell 'em to hire a plumber. But Rita stands there, listening, and tut-tutting in sympathy. In the past, she's actually stopped by to help them out and brought along some homemade blueberry muffins while she's at it. But for some of these folks, even that wasn't enough. The more she'd give, the more they'd want, leaving Rita exhausted and feeling guilty for being exhausted. Still, Rita had a hard time putting on the brakes.

Finally, Smitty and the crew came up with a solution. Now, if Rita's spending too much time with one customer, they'll tell her she's needed out back, and someone else takes over the sale. Works like a charm. Every now and then, we need a little help, you know, to save us from ourselves. (At least, that's what Charlie told me when I discovered he'd eaten the last piece of pecan pie. The piece that I'd been thinking about all day.)

Caitlin's New Age Nook: Compost It

As you know, I work down to Mahoosuc Health Food, and, being in the service industry, I come into contact with all types. The hardest people to deal with are those who are feeling unhappy and powerless in their lives, so they decide to spread those feelings around by taking advantage of the fact that the customer is always right. You've seen or dealt with folks like this—people who think of a sales clerk as a captive audience. I try to feel compassion for these "first lifers," but it's not always easy.

So, I've come up with a visualization that helps. When dealing with a problem customer, first I imagine an energy shield around me for protection. Then, I picture their bad attitude hitting that shield and sliding to the ground. As the you-know-what starts to pile up, I visualize it turning into rich, composted soil. Once the customer leaves, I take a moment to visualize healthy plants growing out of that soil, bearing vegetables or blossoming into beautiful flowers. Having a mental way to transform ugly energy into something beautiful is very satisfying, and gives me closure so I don't take it out on the next customer.

Aunt Ida Tweaks It

Great exercise, but I like to do something more physical. I'm not always good at visualizing. At the A&P, Chip showed us some fun ways to deal with the bad feelings that come from cranky customers. (He did get a few worthwhile things out of his fancy-schmancy education.)

In the employee break room, we have a helium tank and some balloons. When you've had a particularly nasty encounter, instead of taking it out on the next customer, you go out back and blow up a balloon. Then you think about the bad

> *During our Friday-morning meeting, Chip asks us each to draw a picture of our worst customer that week. (We don't name names because Mahoosuc Mills, you remember, is a small town.) Then we go out back to the fire pit, throw in our pieces of paper, and burn the bad customers in effigy.*

energy your customer put on you, really feel it, let it build up, then release that crap by popping the balloon with a straight pin.

Also, during our Friday-morning meeting, Chip asks us each to draw a picture of our worst customer that week. (We don't name names because Mahoosuc Mills, you remember, is a small town.) Then we go out back to the fire pit, throw in our pieces of paper, and burn the bad customers in effigy. This may sound drastic, but it's not. Because the whole exercise is so silly, we all just end up laughing. Took me a while to realize maybe that was the point.

Selling "You-Know-What on a Stick"

Do you have a hobby or something that you love to do? Is there a way you can use it to pick up a little extra pin money? Like Irene, I'm good with numbers, so I moonlight doing books for Smitty's Hardware and the Mahoosuc Mills Mainely Maine store. I wouldn't want to work full-time as a bookkeeper, because I like being out in the public. But as a side job it's great. Plus, I enjoy shopping, so any extra money comes in handy.

I don't believe in quitting your day job and trying to make a living with your hobby. Not right away, anyways. Making a move like that before your business is ready can put a lot of pressure on the things you love: your family, your lifestyle, and your hobby. Plus, you run the risk of turning something you love into just another thing that drags you down. However, starting a little side business, building it up (if you want), and slowly cutting back on hours at your day job can be a good approach. Or, like me, you might want to keep it small and manageable. Just a little extra cash on the side. Nothing wrong with that.

Celeste has it down. She's a whiz-bang at chair caning. Loves it! So, she teaches a couple classes a year down to adult ed at Moose Megantic High. Then she picks up extra money finishing the chairs that her students start (take it from me, chair caning's not for everyone). She has quite a backlog of chairs in her barn. Celeste calls it "the bank." She works through 'em at her own pace, and seems to finish one whenever she needs a little extra cash.

Now as you can imagine, we have quite a few "cottage industries" centered around the tourist trade here in Mahoosuc Mills. Everyone is tryin' to dream up that one good thing folks from away will buy.

If you've visited our great state of Maine, you've seen 'em, I'm sure: lobster-trap coffee tables, chain-saw sculptures, whirligigs, and whatnot. For your more higher-end stuff, our Mainely Maine store is the place. They carry a nice assortment of handmade quilts, braided rugs, balsam pillows, and pine-cone-shaped stuff out the wazoo.

Come June, our town hosts the annual Mahoosuc Mills Blackfly Festival, and a lot of us locals set up booths and tables on Main Street, trying to sell stuff to tourists. Don't matter if we have any talent or not (and to be perfectly honest with you, a lot of us don't). It's just fun to see what folks from away will actually buy.

During the festival, we have an informal contest to see which one of us can come up with the most popular "you-know-what

> *During the festival, we have an informal contest to see which one of us can come up with the most popular "you-know-what on a stick."*

on a stick." What is that, you may ask? It's some hokey-looking geegaw that you buy at a craft fair or festival, something that's too big to fit in a bag, so the buyer has to carry it around, proclaiming to all the world that they actually spent money for this thing.

True "you-know-what on a stick" is not lugged around the festival by a woman. No, she needs to be unencumbered, to check out the beaded jewelry, hand-painted cards, and whatnot. If you're uncertain about whether or not you're witnessing a "you-know-what on a stick" moment, here's a tip: Just look for a wife who's flitting from booth to booth, sampling fudge and chattering away to her husband, who's shuffling along, five paces behind her, trying not to poke someone's eye out with a giant blackfly made out of recycled beer cans. The wife is in her element, having the time of her life, and her husband's hanging in there, hoping that maybe she'll appreciate his effort and he'll get lucky that evening. Or, at the very least, she'll let him have a sausage-and-pepper sub and some fried dough, which are usually off limits on account of his high cholesterol.

Our most famous "you-know-what on a stick" creation was a lawn ornament made by Sally and Ed Jordon. It was written up in both the Bangor and Portland papers and featured on that TV show, *207*. It's been more than ten years since they first come up with it, but the darn things still sell like hotcakes.

How to describe it? Well, you know those lawn ornaments with a woman bending over and all you see is her big butt and polka-dot panties? Sally and Ed decided to create a male version featuring a guy bent over with his jeans hanging low to expose his ample plumber's crack. Sally come up with the idea, and Ed made it (I believe he posed for it, too). They call their creation "Aroostook County Cleavage."

This year's winner, hands down, was Connie LeBlanc's scarecrow clown lawn ornaments. Holy "you-know-what on a stick," Batman! We're talking a *Bride of Chucky* flashback here, folks. Them clowns of hers were positively demonic! Looks like they're going to come to life during the night and eat your young. The darned things are about four feet tall, not including the part that goes in the ground. Connie must have sold a hundred of 'em at twenty bucks a pop! Picture it: a hundred scary clowns, bobbing through the crowd. It's a sight that would have done Stephen King proud!

Gettin' Going

- If you find yourself feeling resentful at work, stop and make a conscious decision to slip it into neutral. Try to coast there for the rest of the day, or the next hour, or five minutes.
- Say to yourself, "If I've got to be here, I might as well be here."
- Try looking people in the eye when you're talking to them. Notice how connecting with folks perks up your energy.
- Focus on what you like about your work. If your mind starts to wander back to things you don't like, bring it back to what you do.
- Spend ten minutes (set a timer) and write down what *success* looks like to you—don't think, just write. You don't have to use complete sentences. Go for it! You may be surprised by the answers.

- Start exploring other work options if you don't like your job. Ask your friends and family what kind of things you're good at or what you seem happy doing.
- Consider coming up with a hobby or things you like doing that could help you earn a little pin money. Is there something you could teach at your local adult ed? One of the best ways to energize your work life is to have things outside of work that you love to do. If you can make a little extra money doing those things, all the better.

Eight

I Can't Die Today

Every year, the male moose sheds his antlers, then grows a new pair. When those antlers emerge, they're covered in a fuzzy coating called "velvet." The moose rubs his antlers against trees and such to work that velvet off. In doing our research, Caitlin found Dr. Nikki (the Internet is a wonderous thing), a totem expert, who said that the rubbing of the antlers represents a "mental housecleaning."

Now, we can certainly learn a lot from a moose on this one. I love this idea, and I know it to be true. If you're feeling stuck, overwhelmed, unable to see the forest for the trees, decluttering your house and/or your mind will put things on an even keel again.

I know if I'm feeling out of sorts, one of the best ways to get myself back on track is to clean house. This works if I'm trying to make a decision or find a solution to a problem, too. There is something about putting things in order, maybe cleaning out a drawer or two, that really works for me. While I distract myself with the task at hand, the back part of my mind is freed up to do its thing without me interfering.

> *If world leaders did their own housecleaning, this would be a more peaceful planet. It's hard to wage war while you're cleaning the toilet.*

I'll be dusting the living room and all of a sudden it comes to me: That blue blouse I got at the Fashion Bug last spring would be perfect with my brand new slacks! Or I'm sorting through my lingerie drawer, and I get this blinding flash of insight: If world leaders did their own housecleaning, this would be a more peaceful planet. It's hard to wage war while you're cleaning the toilet.

I Can't Die Today Because If Anyone Saw the State of My House I'd Die

My house is pretty much tidy and well-kept, although not like my mother's or my grandmother's, of course. Their houses were spotless: knickknacks free of dust, floors clean enough to eat off of, rugs vacuumed, bathrooms fresh as a daisy. Cobwebs? I never saw one inside the house growing up. My mother even had a special little brush she used to comb the fringe on the area rugs—I kid you not.

These were good Franco-American women, women who, if you paused long enough, would clear the dishes off the table while you were still eating. They were that eager to get the kitchen picked up. And they did their spring cleaning (or grand ménage, as they called it) every year, top to bottom, never fail. I don't know anyone who spring-cleans like that anymore. I mean, moving the furniture to vacuum underneath, taking the pictures off the walls and wiping them down, washing the walls and ceilings, even taking everything out of every cabinet and drawer and washing it, plus cleaning the entire stove and fridge. I've probably forgotten something, but I'm worn out just thinking about it.

Even when my mom got cancer, she still did her spring cleaning. She'd do one room a week, my dad moving the furniture for her. Franco to the core!

> *These were good Franco-American women, women who, if you paused long enough, would clear the dishes off the table while you were still eating.*

I don't go wholehog like they did. I just try to keep things picked up, and the counters and stovetop wiped down. Oh, occasionally the house gets away from me and things escalate to the "I-can't-die-today-because-if-anyone-saw-the-state-of-my-house-I'd-die" kind of dirty. But not for long, 'cause it drives me crazy.

Basically, I vacuum, wash the floors, and clean the bathroom once a week, and dust every couple of weeks. And if someone is coming over, I always freshen up the bathroom and race around the house, making sure it looks good.

Now, I'm not saying I love every minute I spend cleaning, especially vacuuming, which can try my patience. That's because of something I call "Ida's Law of Vacuuming."

You've heard of Murphy's Law, right? "Anything that can go wrong, will go wrong." Well, Ida's Law of Vacuuming is similar. "Anything your vacuum cleaner can catch on, it will catch on." It's so irritating! You just need to reach a little further into that corner of the bathroom, a couple of inches is all, and you can't. Why? Your vacuum cleaner is caught on the edge of the door jam or the rug or something. It's stuck and is stubbornly diggin' in its heels.

Yet as irritating as vacuuming can be, it's worth doing 'cause I like how my house looks when it's done. It just makes me feel more comfortable if someone were to drop by.

Like last week, this guy was coming to repair the oven, which wasn't lighting for some reason, and I found myself scrambling to clean the kitchen before he arrived. I even scrubbed down the inside of the oven while I was eating breakfast, and had the racks in to soak by the time Charlie was ready to leave for work.

As he's going out the door, Charlie says, "Ida, why are you fussing? It's just the stove-repair guy."

"I don't know, Charlie. I wish I could just go with it, but I can't. I'd feel like I was letting my mother down."

I admire people who have a relaxed housekeeping style. I really do. I know someone who keeps a vacuum cleaner in her living room, like a piece of furniture or something. If company drops in unexpected, she says, "Oh, you'll have to excuse the house. I was just in the middle of vacuuming." The thing's been there so long, the last time I visited, I saw cobwebs on the vacuum-cleaner hose.

Then there's the burning-candles-in-the-bathroom trick. That's so guests at a party don't have to turn on the light. It looks like the hosts are going for atmosphere, but really it's a dead giveaway that they didn't have time to clean the bathroom. Everything looks better by candlelight, even dusty baseboards.

Both of these methods are beyond me, but I'm inspired by these folks' ability to work the middle ground. They care what people think, but not enough to get compulsive about housework, so they've found a way around it. And they're comfortable with it. That's the part that's hard for me. I just feel more myself when the house is in order, tidy and clean. It's genetic.

I just hope I don't turn into one of those crazy, old Franco-American ladies like my Tante Laura, my father's sister. Her house and yard were always spotless: lawn mowed a little too short, shrubs sculpted to within an inch of their life. Then she got dementia and started cleaning other people's houses. Tante Laura would come to visit and then disappear. We'd find her cleaning the bathroom or sweeping the garage. Her neighbors were at a ball game one time and left the back door unlocked, so Tante Laura let herself in and started cleaning. She took the finish off their stovetop, scrubbing it with steel wool. Folks in her neighborhood finally had to get an injunction against her because if Tante Laura felt they weren't mowing their lawns short enough, or their shrubs needed pruning, she'd do it for them. Poor dear.

Tidy in Mahoosuc Mills Is . . .

- The Subway sandwich shop. Owned by the St. Cyr's, it's not unusual to go in there on any given day and find an employee/family member wiping down the plastic plants and vacuuming the booths.
- Gladys Knight. Not Gladys Knight of Gladys Knight and the Pips. I'm talking about Gladys Knight, the Mahoosuc Mills town clerk. She rules the town offices with an iron fist, everything in its place, desk neat as a pin, her sweater set just so, pant legs creased to a knife's edge. Rumor has it Gladys irons her underwear.
- Charlie's toolbox. He may not pick up his socks off the floor, but his toolbox is a thing of beauty. His truck, not so much.

Feng Shui-ing the Double-Wide

When it comes to livin' the good life, your home is key. I'm not talking about having a big fancy place filled with expensive stuff. No, I'm talking about creating a safe, comfortable home, a place to relax and recharge.

Have you ever walked into someone's house and it looks beautiful, yet feels kind of cold? Or they've lived there for years and the place still feels unsettled? Then there are folks who seem to be barricaded in with shrubs and stuff? These places tend to feel like a house not a home, or a castle instead of a sanctuary.

> *"Feng shui is the ancient Chinese art of organization of a space to facilitate the optimum flow of chi, or life energy." Or as Charlie says, "Arranging furniture to make the worst possible use of the available space."*

Caitlin claims it has to do with energy. And she should know, because she's a certified feng shui consultant. You've heard of feng shui, right? Like what Marie Kondo is doing on her show, "Tidying Up."

I didn't know anything about feng shui when Caitlin first got interested about ten years back. So, I watched a show about it on HGTV, but it's still hard for me to explain. So, I asked Caitlin to make me up a little card so I could brag about her. I keep it in my wallet.

"Feng shui is the ancient Chinese art of organization of a space to facilitate the optimum flow of chi, or life energy." Or as Charlie says, "Arranging furniture to make the worst possible use of the available space." I say anything that makes you stop and think about what you want out of life, which is apparently a big part of feng shui, can't be half bad.

When Caitlin got back from her certification course, I hired her to Feng Shui our double-wide. I wanted to help her get her business started. (Though to be honest, feng shui hasn't exactly caught on in Mahoosuc Mills the way we'd hoped.)

158

Charlie was a little skeptical of the whole thing, so I scheduled my feng shui appointment for Sunday evening, while Charlie was playing poker down to the Brew Ha-Ha with Bud, Smitty, Pat, Tommy, and Junior.

Charlie knew Caitlin was coming, though. As he's going out the door, he says, "Now, listen—I don't want to come home and find some big Buddha statue in the living room, okay?"

"Don't worry, dear. We'll put the Buddha in the backyard beside the fountain and the fish pond you're going to have to put in!"

Well, Caitlin arrived and, God love her, she was so professional. First off, we sat on the floor in what they call the lotus position, except I could only do a half-lotus, and only for about thirty seconds before my hip kind of seized up.

> *First off, we sat on the floor in what they call the lotus position, except I could only do a half-lotus, and only for about thirty seconds before my hip kind of seized up.*

So, we did a centering meditation, Caitlin in the lotus position and me sitting in a chair. Then we talked about my "intentions"—you know, things I want to "manifest." It all sounds kind of silly when I talk about it now, but at the time, I really got into it.

Next Caitlin got out this energy map. It was fascinating. Apparently, different sections of the house represent different areas of your life: relationships, health, family, travel. We were doing pretty good, too, until we got to the wealth area, which, in my house, is located in the bathroom. Swear to God, our wealth is in the toilet.

I says to Caitlin, "This can't be good."

"Well, Aunt Ida, it's not neccesarily the best feng shui. But the good news is, I can give you some basic cures to prevent your wealth from going down the drain."

"Just tell me what to do."

"Well, you might want to buy some plush, green towels. Green symbolizes wealth. And you have to make sure you keep the lid of the toilet closed."

"The towels are easy. But how am I going to explain to Charlie that not only does he have to put the seat down, now he has to remember the lid?"

"I'll give you a crystal to put in your relationship area to enhance communication."

"Well, make it a big one; I don't think Charlie hears half of what I say." (Which reminds me, I need to give Caitlin a call, because I think that crystal needs a tune-up.)

Distract with Sweetness, then Drive a Hard Bargain

One of the most important parts of feng shui is clearing the house of clutter. Energy can't work up a head of steam if it's loaded down with flotsam and jetsam. In Maine, we call decluttering "havin' a yard sale."

I just love yard sales! I love going to 'em and I love having 'em. Because the thing is, if you go to a lot of yard sales, you have to have a yard sale every once in a while to get rid of all the stuff you bought at the other yard sales. Charlie and me have one every few years. June is a good month for yard sales in our neck of the woods.

I've learned through experience that having a successful yard sale is about marketing and product placement. I'd suggest taking out an ad in the local newspaper, and if you live near a big

160

city, like Bangor or Waterville, get an ad in that paper, too. Then you'll get folks from away, and you can charge more.

You need something snappy in your ad to get folks' attention. Here's mine: "If you saw something you liked on the Home Shopping Network that you wished you'd bought but didn't, most likely I did, and I'll be selling it on Saturday. Yard Sale 8–3. Collectibles, furniture, tools, all sorts of bargains. Early birds welcome."

See, I started with the bit about the Home Shopping Network. That's the hook. That's what gets them to read more. Then you have to say you have collectibles because that's trendy. And if you don't think you have them, you do, 'cause everything is collectible to someone. I've seen *Antiques Roadshow*.

Furniture is important. You need a few big pieces to draw people in, make 'em stop and get out of their car. It's not worth your time to have a jelly-jar yard sale. That's when there's a couple tables with lots of little trinkets on them. You'll just get drive-bys with those. A car will slow down, checking out your stuff, and then drive on to the next yard sale on their list.

If you don't have any furniture that you're ready to part with, just have your husband lug out a chest of drawers, a desk, or a trunk—anything big. Then, put a few things on them that are for sale. People will stop to look at the furniture, and when they ask what the price is, you say, "Oh, I'm sorry, deah. That's not for sale. I'm just using it to display those collectibles."

Now, tools. I'm not big on them myself, but you need to put them in your ad for three reasons.

Number one, it might get your husband to tidy up the shed.

Number two, it keeps him occupied, so he's there when you need him to carry heavy things out to a car or truck.

Number three, it's a code. It lets you women know that there's going to be something at the yard sale to occupy your husband, so you can really look around. Plus, then he's there when you need him to lug stuff.

You have to make sure your yard-sale signs are fresh and new. You can make them by hand if you want, or use the ones that the newspaper gives you for taking out the ad. Just don't put up old ones. Then it looks like you're one of those places that's having a permanent yard sale. You've seen 'em: a house with lots of junk piled up in the yard all summer long, yard-sale signs all weather-beaten 'cause they've been out for years, blue tarps everywhere. I stopped at one once where they were trying to sell little packets of mustard and catsup like you get at

> *These people bought newspapers, planned their route to include you, and got up in the middle of the night in order to buy stuff. You have to respect that kind of dedication.*

McDonald's. I mean, come on! They also had half-used boxes of laundry detergent and an old bedpan. Swear to God, an old bedpan!

Now, let me say something about early birds. You know you're going to get them. Why try to fight a force of nature? These people bought newspapers, planned their route to include you, and got up in the middle of the night in order to buy stuff. You have to respect that kind of dedication. If you say your yard sale starts at eight, you can bet you're going to have people lining up at six or six-thirty. Don't start the day off on the wrong foot by getting aggravated at something that's inevitable.

You need to be ready to go by five forty-five. I can't stress this enough. I mean, you have everything priced and displayed, your cash box organized, signs out, hair and makeup done, breakfast eaten, and coffee in a travel mug. This takes planning. In order to have a successful yard sale, you need to spend the week beforehand getting ready.

And when I say "Early birds welcome," I mean it. I have a couple boxes of Dunkin' Munchkins waiting for them, the big box, the one with fifty Munchkins. I'm wearing a smile on my face, lip gloss, and a power bra. These are people from away looking for a deal out in the country, and I am ready to dicker. My motto is: Distract them with sweetness, then drive a hard bargain.

If you're not up for the work of having a yard sale, there are other decluttering options: sell clothes at a consignment shop, or take them and other things you don't use to a thrift store, Goodwill, Salvation Army, or the swap shop down to the dump. Some churches have missions to poor countries or places that have had a natural disaster. The very stuff that's weighing you down could be put to good use by people who really need it. Bottom line: If you want more good things in your life, you have to make room for 'em. And if you help others in the process, so much the better. It's a feel-good all the way 'round.

Once It Leaves the House, It Doesn't Come Back In

The Golden Rule of Yard Sales is: Once it leaves the house, it doesn't come back in. Ever!

One way to keep the Golden Rule is to remember this key point: If an item has any sentimental value—I don't care if it's a bottle cap—keep it. If you remember that, holding firm to the Golden Rule is easy, and you'll be ready to part with everything in your yard sale.

That means at the end of the day, whatever hasn't sold gets sorted into two piles: dump and Goodwill. It's just common sense. After making all that effort to get rid of the stuff, why the heck would you haul it back inside to collect dust for another ten years? This is why your yard sale only goes until three o'clock. That gives you time to sort through the stuff that didn't sell, drop some at Goodwill, haul the rest to the dump, and still make it to the baked bean supper down to the Congo Church in time to get a piece of peanut butter pie.

Besides, you know your stuff will be appreciated by the folks at Goodwill and by Whitey Hebert down to the dump. I'm sure you got someone like him in your town, too. Just about every weekend, spring through fall, Whitey and his son, Little Whitey, who's got to be over six feet tall and probably weighs 250, are pretty much camped out down to the Swap Shop, waiting to score the stuff that people didn't sell at their yard sales.

> *Whitey Hebert . . . now there's a piece of work. You'll never see him at a yard sale. For a fella like Whitey, buying stuff is out of the question. That would be failing at his life's mission, which is getting stuff for free.*

Whitey Hebert . . . now there's a piece of work. You'll never see him at a yard sale. For a fella like Whitey, buying stuff is out of the question. That would be failing at his life's mission, which is getting stuff for free. No, Whitey backs his truck right up to the Swap Shop at the dump and just stands in the doorway. When he sees you driving up, he's like, "Come to Papa." Your boxes of junk never even hit the ground. They go directly from your truck to his—all of it, he's not picky. And Whitey never breaks a sweat. If there's any heavy lifting to do, Little Whitey does all the work. Whitey Hebert just stands there chewing tobacco and supervising.

Now what does Whitey Hebert do with all that crap from the Swap Shop? Well, I'll tell you. He brings it home, puts it under one of them blue tarps, and your stuff merges into what's got to be one of the moldiest yard sales in Maine. Whitey's wife, June, runs that part of the operation. Poor dear. More days than not, she's sitting in her lawn chair, in a housedress, hair in curlers, smoking a butt. Charlie calls her Our Lady of the Perpetual Yard Sale.

Straight Talk from the Barcalounger: Yard-Sale Pointers

Between you and me, the way to get 'round the Golden Rule of Yard Sales is to never actually take anything out of the shed. If a fella's looking for tools, he can come inside. This bugs Ida no end, but I tell her, "I have to keep an eye on the merchandise. Make sure nobody takes any." Ida thinks all I got in those old shoeboxes is a bunch a rusty junk. But no. What I have are some highly collectible, antique tools.

Here's my sales technique: A fella comes into the shed to check things out. When he finds something he's interested in, I saunter over to him and we stand there, staring at the item in question, shooting the breeze. We talk about the weather, the Red Sox, fishing, the Patriots, last hunting season, the Celtics, next hunting season, whatever, 'til the guy actually refers to the object of his desire. Then I usually say, "Well, I don't know if I'm quite ready to part with that."

We chew the fat some more about the town council meeting last Tuesday, NASCAR, and candlepin bowling, and then the fella makes an offer. And I ask him about his wife, his kids, his dog, and just when I think he's plumb tuckered out, I do the deal. Here's the most important part: Whatever you do, don't make eye contact. Not until you're done dickerin'.

Chunking Things Down into Manageable Pieces

Feeling bogged down in your life? Want to get the energy moving? Decluttering your mind is right up there with decluttering your house, as far as I'm concerned. My rule of thumb: If I find myself thinking about something over and over again, I know it's time to let it go. I only have so much brain space, and this kind of thought-loop is guaranteed to muck up the works. What follows are some tricks I've found to help me declutter my mind.

Make a list. This is the best way I know to make space in my brain. Because I get overwhelmed when I have a lot of things to do—I have a system—I create a big list for the week. Then every morning I look at the big list, write down a few things that are realistic goals for that day, and take the short list with me. I do not drag that big list around with me. If I did that, I wouldn't know where to start. It's just too unwieldy.

> *If I find myself thinking about something over and over again, I know it's time to let it go. I only have so much brain space, and this kind of thought-loop is guaranteed to muck up the works.*

Chunking things down into manageable pieces really helps me get things done, too. For example, if I'm having some folks over to dinner, I make a list of all the stuff I have to do to get ready, then I divide those things into what I'm going to do each day for the five days leading up to the dinner party. On Monday, I dust and plan the menu. Tuesday I do the basic grocery shopping. Wednesday, I clean the stovetop and wipe down the kitchen cabinets. Thursday, I vacuum and pick up the perishable groceries. Friday, I clean the bathroom and make the soup or anything else you can make ahead of time. Finally, on Saturday, the day of the dinner, I'll divide the day into sections and decide what I'm going to do in the morning, afternoon, and right before the guests arrive. Sound like a lot of work? Compared to doing it willy-nilly, it's a dream.

The most important thing about a list? Keep it with you and actually read it. I'm guilty of not doing this. I go to all the trouble of making a list and bringing it with me to the store. But, I think I remember what's on the list, so I don't look at it and forget one of the major ingredients for supper. Only myself to blame; I should know better.

Make a Worry Appointment

We talked about regrets and resentments earlier. They sure can take up a lot of room in your head. Give Caitlin's Regrets Repair Remedy or my tweak a try. I can't stress this enough: Do what you need to do to tidy up the old issues that are keeping you stuck where you are. Let 'em go and move on with your life. Not always easy, but worth the effort.

What were you worrying about six months, six weeks ago, six hours ago? If you're like me, you probably can't remember. Worrying is one of those things that is a complete waste of time, but we do it anyway. My favorite time to worry is in the middle of the

> *What were you worrying about six months ago? If you're like me, you probably can't remember. Worrying is one of those things that is a complete waste of time, but we do it anyway.*

night when I wake up to pee and then spend a fitful hour (or

167

more) mulling things over that I can do nothing about at that moment.

For me, worrying falls into two categories: the big stuff, like world peace and global warming, and the everyday things, like whether my nephew Jimmy will get laid off, or if Charlie will be all right driving to work in the freezing rain. Both the big and everyday things are out of my control, really. But somehow I confuse worrying with actually doing something about it.

To help deal with worry, and this may sound a little weird, I make a worry appointment. Say I'm worried about Jimmy getting laid off from his job at the Forestry Service. He counts trees or something like that. Just loves it, and he's a hell of a good worker, but last one hired, first one fired, right? So, I find myself thinking about Jimmy throughout the week and my stomach starts churning every time I do. That's a waste of time and energy.

So I say to myself, "Okay, Ida. You can worry like crazy about Jimmy on Friday between 4:30 and 5:30." That's when he gets out of work and picks up his paycheck. If he gets a pink slip, he'll call his mother, my sister Irene, and she'll call me. Anytime during the week when I find myself starting to worry about Jimmy's job, I remind myself, "Not now. You can worry all you want on Friday." That way I still feel like I'm doing my part, showing I care by worrying about Jimmy, but I'm keeping it to an hour. That frees up a lot of brain space.

Many times, I'll set a worry appointment and by the time I get to it, the thing I was going to worry about has already passed, so I skip the worrying altogether. For example, my dad got pneumonia a couple of years ago, so now every time he gets a cold, I'm concerned it'll escalate. Say I talk to him on a Wednesday, and he's come down with a bad cold. I think, I'm not going to worry about pneumonia until Monday. Sometimes I have to remind myself every other minute about not worrying until then, but it's worth it. When Monday arrives and he's feeling better, I never think, Darn! Now I'm not going to get to worry.

Another way to take your worrying down a notch is to think "What if?" What if the thing I'm worrying about happens? What if my dad gets pneumonia? We'll deal with it, right? We've all had bad things happen, but somehow, we make it through. And we'll continue to roll with whatever comes our way because we always have. It may feel weird, but by asking yourself, "What would I do if the worst happens?", you will realize that you could handle it. Once you realize that, the knot in your stomach and the clenching around your heart relaxes and the worry lessens.

Caitlin's New Age Nook:
Twenty-Seven Feels like Heaven
In feng shui, nine is an auspicious number, so we try to do things in multiples of nine. If you're feeling stuck in your life and want to get the energy moving, give away one thing a day for twenty-seven days. This is a pretty standard feng shui exercise. Lots of experts recommend it. That's because it works. As you give away the things that are no longer of use to you, set the intention that you're making room for new things that you want: new clothes, a new job, a new relationship, happiness.

Aunt Ida Tweaks It
Giving one thing away a day for twenty-seven days certainly is manageable. But, I like to move things along a little faster. Besides, I'm not going to the Goodwill every day, and can't stand driving around with a bunch of giveaway stuff in my car for days on end. So I do the

Twenty-Seven Feels like Heaven in one day. If you're speedy, you can get this done in an hour or less. Plus, it'll count as your aerobic workout.

I call it "Chuck it in the Bucket." Get a bucket, laundry basket, or garbage bag and quickly go around the house, attic, basement, drawers, jewelry box, whatever, and grab stuff that you haven't used in a year, clothes that don't fit, things you never liked. When you get at least twenty-seven, stop and sort the stuff into throwaway, giveaway, bring to a thift store, and sell on consignment. Then put that stuff into your car and take it where it needs to go. Do not drive around for more than a week with this junk. That's just moving the clutter from one place to another. Give it away. It's very liberating!

Gettin' Going

- Clean your house, a room, or a drawer to get unstuck. Cleaning won't solve all your problems, but worst case, things'll be tidy.
- Create a list to organize your schedule. If you already use a list, but are still not getting things done, try making a smaller daily list.
- Chunk down big jobs into more manageable pieces. If you're having a hard time figuring out how to do this, ask a friend. Sometimes a fresh eye is all you need.
- Make a worry appointment. Or ask yourself, "What if the thing I'm worried about actually happens? Then what?"

Nine

Listening to Your Inner Moose

Caitlin says to me, "Aunt Ida, in your book, you're going to do a chapter on intuition, right?"

"Oh, I don't think so, Caitlin," I reply.

"But tuning in to your intuition is another tool you can use to improve your quality of life."

"That's seems a little too woo-woo for me."

"Well," Caitlin says, "intuition means listening to what your inner voice is telling you about people and situations. That can help you avoid potiential problems and disappointments. Sounds like living the good life to me."

"But I don't know anything about intuition," I say.

"You use your intuition all the time, Aunt Ida."

"Do not."

"Do, too. How many times have I heard you say, 'I had a hunch' or 'I felt like I should call so-and-so to check in, and it turned out they were home sick in bed'?"

"Well, usually there was something about the person that just didn't seem right the last time I saw 'em. I'm just paying attention."

"Right! You're paying attention. That's what intuition is all about."

Once I started thinking about it like that, I realized that using your intuition isn't this big mysterious thing. It's nothing more than tuning in to your senses and trusting what they tell you.

Surprisingly, we can learn a lot from a moose on this one. They have a wicked sharp sense of smell and hearing and excellent depth perception, and they use these senses to keep themselves safe. Paying attention to our senses can do the same for you and me, too.

Seems All Right to Me

My grandmother, Dora Gilbert, used to freeze her garbage. This was in the days before garbage disposals, so there was a lot to freeze. But she didn't let that intimidate her. For Dora, freezing garbage was more than just a way to keep it from stinking. It was an art form. I can see my grandmother now standing in her immaculate kitchen, a little Franco-American woman with permed gray hair, full makeup, a housedress, nylon stockings, sensible shoes, and a bib apron, carefully wrapping her garbage in little foil packets and tucking them into the freezer.

There's nothing unusual about freezing garbage; not in my family, anyway. We all freeze our garbage. Having a garbage disposal doesn't really make a difference, 'cause there are always things that you can't put down the disposal, such as lobster shells, banana peels, and the like. Even Caitlin, who does composting, freezes her garbage until it's time to bring it out to the compost bin in her backyard.

By now you're thinking OCD, right? Or at the very least, Felix from *The Odd Couple*? It's not that my family is compulsively neat (though we certainly are tidy). It's just that, for whatever reason, all the women in my family have a heightened sense of smell.

At times, it can be downright debilitating. When a person sitting close to me in the movie theater has on too much perfume, I have to change seats. Heck, I get woozy to the point of passing out if I smell spoiled food, and I live in fear of being sprayed by a skunk. I seriously don't believe I could survive it. Cause of death: olfactory overload.

Conversely, Charlie can't smell anything. He's not running with the moose on this one. Why he hasn't died of food poisoning is beyond me. God knows, I try to keep our fridge cleaned out, but as I've learned many times, perfection is elusive. Tupperware has a way of migrating to the back of the shelf, then out of my memory altogether. Or, I'll make a recipe that calls for six ounces of ricotta, which only comes in an eight-ounce container. So, of course, the remaining two ounces gets put in the fridge, where it hides, gestating. Gives me the willies!

I'll walk into the kitchen and see Charlie scarfing down something.

"What are you eating?" I ask.

"Some of that chili you made."

"Charlie, that's been in there for a week and a half!"

He just shrugs. "Seems all right to me."

"You, mister man, are going to end up in the emergency room someday."

His response is always the same: "Ain't happened yet."

But, as disgusting as the stench of life can be, it's worth the gagging to be able to have the good smells: sheets fresh from the line, the top of a baby's head, lilacs in the spring, cookies baking in the oven. Our little dog, Scamp, smells like sunshine, optimism, and unconditional love (well, most of the time, anyways). Then there's new-mown grass, furniture polish, coffee, bacon, and Charlie. Even when Charlie doesn't smell so good, he smells good to me.

Smell is so important to me that whenever I hear myself say, "Something about that doesn't smell right," or "that situation smells fishy to me," I sit up and take notice. Now I know, that's my intuition telling me to pay attention.

Straight Talk from the Barcalounger:
Go with Your Gut

If my head's telling me one thing and my gut another, I go with my gut. The way I figure it, my gut's bigger than my head, so it must be right.

Your head can talk you into anything. Been there. Done that. But your gut doesn't lie.

If more people paid attention to their gut, the world would be a better place. I'm just saying.

Spousal Deafness

Now if you were a fly on the wall of our double-wide, you'd think Charlie was deaf as a post, but he's not. I discovered what his real problem was a few years back when he had to go in for a physical for his new insurance at work. He hadn't been in a dog's age.

Before Charlie left, I told him to make sure they tested his hearing, 'cause as far was I was concerned, he seemed to be having a problem in that area. When he gets home, he's pleased as punch to report that his hearing is perfect. I say, "That must mean you're suffering from spousal deafness. It's only me you can't hear."

"What?" he replies.

See, I'd taken one of them quizzes in *Cosmo*. (Don't know how I ended up with a subscription to that. Must have been that magazine drive the Band Boosters were doing.) I kept it 'cause Charlie got a perfect score.

Spousal Deafness: Real or Imagined

Answer yes or no to the following questions:

Q. Does your spouse say "What?" to almost every thing you say?

A. Yes, and it's irritating as all get out.

Q. Is your spouse unable to remember entire conversations that you have had with him?

A. Yes. It could be something we talked about yesterday or ten minutes ago. It don't matter.

Q. Is your spouse able to hear a complete stranger who is talking in a whisper across the room, yet is unable to hear you when you're sitting across the kitchen table?

A. Yup. He's got some kind of supersonic hearing if someone else is talking. What's up with that?

Q. When you ask your spouse to pick up something you need at the grocery store, something specific, does he say, "Sure," then return with the very thing you didn't want?

A. Yes. Once I even tried cutting out a picture from the newspaper, pasting it onto the list, and he still come home with the wrong thing.

Q. Have you ever given your spouse loving advice over and over again, only to have a friend or even an acquaintance offer the same advice, and watch your spouse act like he's never heard the idea before? When you say, "Honey,

I've told you that a million times," Does your spouse say,
"Really?"

A. Yes. Yes! Yes!!

Conclusion: If you have answered yes to any or all of these
questions, your spouse is exhibiting just some of the symptoms
of spousal deafness.

No shit!

If Charlie'd done that good on his tests in high school,
he'd've gone to Harvard!

Well, then the wicked smart people at *Cosmo* go on to suggest a plan to deal with spousal deafness. They recommend
doing what they call a "creative visualization." I figure, what the
heck! Why not give it a try?

> *So the next thing I know,
> I'm sitting in the den,
> cross-legged, on the shag
> carpet, citronella candles
> all 'round (them was the
> only ones I had), doing
> a creative visualization.
> The magazine said you're
> supposed to burn some
> incense but I didn't have
> any, so I lit up a mosquito
> coil.*

So the next thing I know, I'm
sitting in the den, cross-legged,
on the shag carpet, citronella
candles all 'round (them was the
only ones I had), doing a creative
visualization. The magazine said
you're supposed to burn some
incense but I didn't have any, so I
lit up a mosquito coil. Now what
you're supposed to do is picture
yourself swimming down your
husband's ear canal.

I was going to look up the
structure of the inner ear in the
World Book Encyclopedia. (This is before I became such a computer wiz.) See, Charlie and I have a complete set that we
bought on the installment plan when we were first married (and

I just can't bring myself to part with them). But then I figure, what the heck. They don't call it creative visualization for nothing.

So, I'm swimming down Charlie's ear canal. It looks just like this tropical stream I saw on a commercial once. "Come to Jamaica." The water's that pretty turquoise color. Warm as bathwater. I see Charlie's eardrum in the distance. It's hanging there like some big, old African drum beside this beautiful waterfall. So, I swim up to it and I tap out my message on his eardrum (which is what you're supposed to do): "Charlie, bring home rolled oats, not quick oats. They make the cookies too mushy." Then I think. Geez Louise, I swam all this way. So I tap out. "Charlie, take Ida to Jamaica."

At that point I hear the kitchen door open and slam shut, Charlie throw his keys and lunch bag down on the counter, the refrigerator door open and slam shut, and a Budweiser pop open. I swim back to reality in time to see Charlie coming 'round the corner, propping himself up against the doorjamb, sippin' his Bud.

"What's for supper? I picked up the oats you wanted." Then he gives me that smile. "You making cookies tonight, dear?"

He doesn't even wait for an answer. He just beelines it for the Barcalounger, his hand reaching out, ready to do a little bonding with the remote, when he stops and sniffs and says, "You been using fly dope in here?"

I get up, which sounds easier than it was 'cause my butt and right leg had fallen asleep, and go into the kitchen. And there, sitting on the counter, plain as day, is a container of quick oats.

I did one more creative visualization. I pictured myself canceling my subscription to *Cosmo*.

Being a Good Listener

Truth be told, most of the time, Charlie hears me. He just doesn't want to so he pretends he doesn't. You know the game. And I'd be the first to admit, a lot of things I say aren't worth responding to. However, if it's something important, and we're sitting down together, Charlie gives me his undivided attention. He's a good listener, really. I'm lucky that way. Listening; it's a lost art.

For example, have you ever had a conversation with a person who is so busy thinking about what they're going to say once you finish talking, they're not really listening? Or, how about this one: You're talking to someone, asking 'em questions, finding out all sorts of stuff about them, right? Then you realize twenty minutes have gone by, and they haven't asked you a single thing about yourself? In fact, they haven't exhibited the least bit of interest in you or what you're doing. Kind of makes you feel invisible, doesn't it?

By actively listening, you let the person who's talking know they're important, that you value them. But it's a two-way street. That's why it's called "conversation." Otherwise, it's a monologue, which belongs on a stage, not at a backyard barbecue.

Being a good listener also means not only listening to what's being said, but what's not being said. That includes listening to yourself, too. Are you saying one thing and feeling another? Listen to that. Do you know someone who talks a good game, but their actions say something different? Pay attention to that. Again, it's about tuning in to your senses and trusting what they tell you.

Caitlin's New Age Nook: Listening to Your Inner Voice

Have you ever heard a voice in your head say, "I should call so-and-so," but for whatever reason you don't? Later it turns out that person was really depressed that day, and you wished you'd followed through. Or, a thought pops into your head: "I have to remember to take the umbrella." But you get distracted, forget, and end up wet from running errands all day in the pouring rain with no umbrella.

Try this: Commit to follow through when that little voice tells you something. Try it for an hour, a day, or a week. Once you get the hang of it, you'll find that the voice gets stronger, and life gets easier. Really!

Aunt Ida Tweaks It

Can't argue with this one. Once I started doing it, I got kind of addicted. And now I hardly ever have to turn around when I get to the end of the street, go back to the house, and make sure I shut the iron off—I checked it before I left when that little voice told me to.

Seeing the Whole Picture

Moose have excellent depth perception. I looked that up in the dictionary. (Well, Wikipedia really. Pretty impressive, huh?) "Depth perception," they say, "is the visual ability to see the world in three dimensions."

So the moose, with its finely tuned depth perception, is teaching us to use all our senses to see the whole picture, not just the surface.

I remember once Grampy Gilbert and me were in his canoe when we got socked in with fog. I mean, pea soup. Couldn't see

> *I remember once Grampy Gilbert and me were in his canoe when we got socked in with fog. I mean, pea soup. Couldn't see a thing. I panicked. "What'll we do, Grampy?"*
>
> *"Shhh," he whispers. "Use your nose. Use your ears. You were born with all these senses, ma chère. Use them."*

a thing. I panicked. "What'll we do, Grampy?"

"Shhh," he whispers. "Use your nose. Use your ears. You were born with all these senses, *ma chère*. Use them."

He'd paddle for a while, then stop, and we'd listen and smell, and by and by, I could smell the trees and hear the birds in the trees, the insects buzzing. The shoreline was getting closer. I could feel it.

As Grampy Gilbert used to say, "A good guide knows how to find his way in the woods, and not just with his eyes, either."

Sometimes I'd see Grampy Gilbert close his eyes while fishing, and move his mouth like he was tasting the air. Then, we'd paddle to a different spot and hook a big one. He could feel the change of a breeze and know rain was coming. It was amazing how Grampy had trained himself to use all his senses to see the whole picture.

Your Personal GPS

Grampy Gilbert had this amazing internal compass. He could find his way in the woods without the aid of a map. Grampy had a finely tuned guidance system, and all he had to do was tap into it. I think we all do, but, frankly, sometimes I get lost. I relapse into a jag of people-pleasing. (Hey, it happens.) Once I get on that gerbil wheel, it's hard to get off, and I start losing touch with what I want, what makes me happy, why I'm here.

I know I'm not the only one. At least I hope I'm not. When I'm feeling like this, it's easy to start looking outside of myself for something to give me guidance and make me feel better: Dr. Phil, my horoscope, Ben & Jerry's. I forget that I have an internal guidance system, too.

This hit home a while back when I was working down to the A&P. In comes Claire Lambert with her new baby, Michelle. Cute? Oh, my God! All bundled up in pink, with that twinkle in her eye. Babies always look so wise to me, like they know something we don't. They're like little Yodas. Well, to be honest, some look more like little monkeys, but most look like Yoda (without the wrinkles).

So, I'm looking down at baby Michelle, and she's staring at me with those big dark eyes, and I'm thinking about how wise she looks, when suddenly, I remember something Grampy Gilbert told me years ago. Grampy said that moose calves are born with their eyes wide open. I don't know if he saw that for real, or what, but I went home and looked it up, and it's true. I thought about that, and it come to me that, in a way, maybe we're all born with our eyes open too. If you think about how wise babies look, you gotta wonder if we don't come into this world knowing everything we need to know. Then, somehow, as we grow older and get distracted by the business of life, we forget what we know.

I think that's why it can be so frustrating waiting and hoping for a miraculous lightning bolt to strike and tell you why you're here. Well, what if that lightning bolt is never going to strike, because it already did, before you were born? That would take the pressure off, wouldn't it?

You know Harry Potter with that lightning bolt on his forehead? Well, for the rest of us, I believe the lightning bolt isn't up there. I believe it's in your heart. Your heart knows why you're here. Your heart knows what to do next, how to treat others, how to be good to yourself. All you really need to do is get quiet, check in with your heart, and remember what you were born knowing.

Getting in Touch with Your Senses in Mahoosuc Mills Is . . .

- The smell of balsam fir or a woodstove on a cold winter's day.
- Wild blueberries just picked, with real maple syrup and cream.
- Walkin' in the woods after a rain storm, feelin' the still misty air on my face, smellin' it and listenin' to the birds singin'. I think they think they sound better after it rains. Or hearing the hoot owls callin' to one another at dusk.
- Comin' back from a trip, roundin' the corner and seeing that old sign that reads WELCOME TO MAHOOSUC MILLS.

 Caitlin's New Age Nook: Checking in with Your Heart
Need some guidance to solve a problem or make a decision? Check in with your heart. It only takes ten minutes. Really!

All you need is a piece of paper, a pen, and a timer. Take a quiet minute to become present. Think about the situation, problem, or decision you're seeking guidance for. When you're ready, put your hands over your heart and ask your heart to guide you. Then set the timer for ten minutes and go. Write without stopping. I mean it. Do not think. Do not stop writing. Write whatever comes into your head. Sometimes I find myself writing, "This is stupid. I don't know why I'm doing this," or "I'm hungry. I wonder what I'll have for lunch." When this happens, ask your heart for guidance once again, gently refocus on the problem you're trying to solve, and continue writing. Don't worry about neatness or spelling. It's about getting thoughts out of your head and onto paper. When the timer goes off, stop. Place your hands on your heart and say, "Thank you!"

Then crumple up the paper, throw it away, and get on with your day. Yes, you read that right. Throw it away. You don't even have to read it. If the solution didn't come to you in the writing (sometimes it does, sometimes it doesn't), it will come to you within the next few days. You just need to declutter your mind.

 Aunt Ida Tweaks It
I know this sounds kind of weird, but Caitlin's wicked smart and it does work.
Sometimes when I don't have time to write it all out, I just cut to the chase. I put my hands over my heart and say, "Help!" And when the solution comes, I put my hands over my heart again and say, "Thank you!"

My Dad, the Philosopher

My dad doesn't have a lot of schooling, but if common sense counts, he's a pretty smart guy. Kind of a philosopher, really.

So, I was talking to dad awhile back, you know, checking in. He's slowing down some. He doesn't play golf or bowl anymore, and he'd stopped doing a lot of activities down to Mahoosuc Green. But, last winter he got new hearing aids, and we realized he wasn't doing things because he couldn't hear good. Now he can, and he's been going to Bingo (which he calls Beano) and concerts.

He even joined the men's group. When I asked what they do, he says they sit around and talk about how to make the place better, which sounds about right for a men's group.

"There are some guys there," he says, "nothing's ever right. My feeling is, this is a nice place and I'm lucky to have the life I have. Besides, when I moved in here, I made up my mind I was just going to go with the flow. Makes life easier."

"What did you do this week, dad?" I ask.

"Oh, you know, beano. Went to a movie in the movie room."

"What'd you see?"

"Can't remember, but the popcorn was good. Oh, and I went to a program about end of life."

"You did? What was it like?

"They asked us questions, and folks shared stuff. It was interesting."

"What kind of questions?"

"Like, 'If you had twenty-four hours to live, what would you do?'"

I immediately started thinking about what I'd eat, which tells you something about me.

"What'd you say, dad?"

"I said I'd make my bed because that's the only thing I have left undone."

You know, that sounds like a joke, but if you stop and really think about it, wow! It's deep.

I'm inspired by dad, and am aiming to be as content with my life as he is. I believe listening to my inner voice is going to help me get there.

Gettin' Going

- Pay attention to your senses when you take a walk. What do you hear and smell? How does the breeze feel on your face—the sun, the grass beneath your feet?
- Decide to really listen to someone you love. Listen to what's being said and tune in to what's not being said.
- Take notice if you're getting a weird feeling from someone, or something.
- Having trouble making a decision? Decide to do it, and spend a day seeing how that feels. Then make the decision not to do it. How does that feel? Go with the one that feels best.
- Commit to listening to your inner voice, and to following through. Amazing things will happen!

Ten

Getting Rid of Frogs and Toads

When was the last time you hung around doing nothin'? I mean, just lollygaggin' about, watching the day go by? The older you get, the tougher that is to pull off. There's always something that needs to be done—always! Why, even vacations tend to be jam-packed.

I remember being a kid, whinin' to my mother, "Mom, I'm bored! There's nothin' to do!" This was back in the days before kids were plugged in, before they spent their summers going to science camp, hockey camp, gymnastics camp, and so on. Summer was just an endless string of long, hot days spent outside with friends, playing hide-and-seek and riding bikes from house to house (without helmets, of course).

We'd make tents by hanging old blankets on the clothes-line and staking them down with rocks. Then we'd put more blankets inside. No matter how hot it was, me, Irene, and our friends used to lie about in our tent for hours, reading *Archie* comic books, drinking orange Kool-Aid, and eating Oreos.

Now my days are filled with gottas. Gotta do this. Gotta do that. And I know I'm not the only one.

The other day, my friend Celeste and me were gabbing on the phone, catching up on things, and, as usual, talking about our husbands. She says, "Ida, sometimes I just snap at Bud for no good reason. I feel bad after. Heck, I feel bad while I'm doing it, but I just can't help myself!"

"I know what you mean," I say. "There are some days when every time I open my mouth to say something to Charlie, only frogs and toads come out. Nothing but frogs and toads."

"Why is that, Ida? They're both sweet guys."

"I've come to the conclusion that multitasking makes us cranky," I say. "See, these guys have the luxury of only doing one thing at a time. Us women are responsible for keeping an eye on the Big Picture. We're going in a million different directions, getting pulled this way and that way. Why, we have so many balls in the air, all it takes is a feather added to the mix and we snap."

Celeste agreed. Then she had to go because she was babysitting her grandson, Robbie, had a pie in the oven, and needed to take in the laundry off the line before it started to rain.

I read an article that said multitasking was an inefficient way of doing things. Of course, it was written by a man. Hello! Try making supper without multitasking! "Here you go, Charlie. Once we've eaten our fill of meat loaf, I'll start peeling the potatoes."

I used to blame that overwhelmed feeling on PMS, then peri-menopause, then menopause, but, as I said earlier, things have pretty much settled down in that department. So basically, all my excuses for being short-tempered with Charlie are gone. That's what I was thinking as I sat in my craft room, doing a little deep breathing. I'd just about snapped his head off for asking me if we had any pickled eggs left, so I'd given myself a time-out.

See, we were going to a potluck at Rita and Smitty's, and I was trying out a new recipe I'd gotten from Franny Lefebvre, a faux Lobster Thermidor made with them Sea Legs. I'd had it at the Knights of Columbus summer picnic and it was delicious! Franny was nice enough to share her recipe. "It's easy!" she said, and wrote it down on a cocktail napkin, but I was having a hard time reading her handwriting. I was trying to decide whether the recipe called for a half-cup of light cream or one and a half cups, when the phone starts ringing. Charlie doesn't even make a move to answer. No, he's "busy" looking for pickled eggs in the fridge, meaning he's opened the door and is just standing there, staring. Not moving a thing, mind you, just staring into the fridge.

> *I was trying to decide whether the recipe called for a half-cup of light cream or one and a half cups, when the phone starts ringing. Charlie doesn't even make a move to answer. No, he's "busy" looking for pickled eggs in the fridge, meaning he's opened the door and is just standing there, staring. Not moving a thing, mind you, just staring into the fridge.*

"Do we have any of them pickled eggs left?" he asks me as I'm wiping off my hands so I can answer the phone. I opened my mouth and, you guessed it—frogs and toads.

Now, if I'd asked him to get the phone, he would have, but you'd think he'd be able to figure that out on his own. I know I should delegate more, but asking, explaining, and checking to see if it's done right is just too time-consuming. It's quicker doing it myself. Plus, my problem is, I wait too long to ask for help. By the time I say "uncle" my head feels like it's about to pop off.

An hour later, when I get into the car, where Charlie has been sitting waiting for me for ten minutes, I say, "Tell you what, mister man—next time *you* can rush around the house pulling the curtains, shutting the lights, making sure the iron is off, putting aluminum foil on the Lobster Thermidor, and getting Scamp settled for the evening, while I wait in the car with the motor running!"

"Hey," he says, "I put the beer in the cooler and came out here to cool down the car so you wouldn't ruin your new outfit." Then he looks at me and smiles. "Pink sure is a pretty color on you, Ida."

Well, needless to say, it would have taken a lot more energy to stay cranky at that moment than to just let it go. I admit, Charlie has learned a thing or two in forty years of marriage.

What I've learned is that if I don't take time to recharge and reenergize myself, I have nothing left to give Charlie or anyone else. It's not unlike my mom and dad looking after their relationship first, so they could be there for us girls. Livin' the good life means putting myself at the top of my priority list every once in a while. If I don't, before I know it, I'm knee-deep in frogs and toads. Do not let this happen to you. Head off those slimy things at the pass by looking out for number one.

Nourishing Your Inner Spirit in Mahoosuc Mills Is . . .

- Hearing the Sisters of St. Joseph sing hymns in French at 7:00 mass, on Christmas Eve. Always makes me cry, it's so beautiful!
- Any food from when I was a kid, like a toasted cheese sandwich with Campbell's tomato soup, or a fried baloney cup (fried baloney, filled with a scoop of mashed potato and topped with some creamed corn) or penny candy.

- Charlie and me up to Dot and Tommy's camp, just the two of us at sunrise, sitting on the end of the dock, mist rising off the water, the lake like glass, watching the day begin.

Erotic Dessert

Now you wouldn't think we could learn much from a moose on this one, but we can. This is wicked interesting! A moose is a mammal, right? But did you know they can feed at the bottom of a lake for up to a minute? It's true! Then they swim to the surface, still chomping away on the tasty green stuff they find down there.

"Kinda like a moose salad bar!" Caitlin says.

"Right," I says. "But what can we learn from this?"

"You mean, besides eat your leafy greens?"

"Yeah. Let's think about it. The moose has the ability to dive deep and return with nourishment."

"Which, Aunt Ida, could also mean taking the time to nourish yourself, to reconnect and reenergize."

"Bingo!"

Now, some people run or huff and puff down to the gym (God bless 'em!). Some, like Caitlin, do yoga and meditate (my hat's off to them, too). But I don't think reconnecting with yourself and reenergizing has to be that involved. It could be as simple as knitting, singing in the shower, or reading a trashy novel. (I don't go in for the heavy stuff. My feeling is, why do I need to read *The Beans of Egypt, Maine* when I could take a ride down any number of dirt roads outside of Mahoosuc Mills and experience it firsthand?) Even better, read a trashy novel while taking a hot bath! That usually works.

Heck, let's quit beating around the bush. For reenergizing and nourishing your inner spirit there's nothing quite as effective as eating something you love. Am I right?

Now, I'm not talking about wolfing down a pint of Ben & Jerry's in the middle of the night, directly from the carton while standing at the kitchen sink, then hiding the empty container at the bottom of the trash can. (Not that any of us have ever done such a thing.)

No, I'm talking about taking the time to eat your favorite food with gusto, without guilt, preferably with a friend or two. The Women Who Run with the Moose do this kind of thing all the time. Some of us are into bread—that would be Dot. Betty and Celeste like crunchy, salty things like chips and nuts. But for me, Rita, and Shirley, it's dessert.

> *Have you ever had a dessert that's so good you find yourself dreaming about it the next day, maybe even weeks or months after? So good that you stand there, staring into space, as you relive each tasty bite?*

Tell me, have you ever had a dessert that's so good you find yourself dreaming about it the next day, maybe even weeks or months after? So good that you stand there, staring into space, as you relive each tasty bite? You start neglecting other desserts, desserts you've had a long and happy relationship with, in favor of the flat-out lust you feel for this dreamy new confection. If that's the case, my friends, you've found what I refer to as an "erotic dessert."

Last spring, Celeste, Rita, Betty, Dot, Shirley, and me went to Bangor for a day of shopping. We had coupons for Macy's and the Michael's Craft Store, plus, they were having a big sale at Super Shoes.

So, us girls drive to Bangor and spend the day browsing around and trying on clothes and buying craft supplies. We all have lunch at Bugaboo Creek. By three o'clock, we were shopped out. We all crawl back into Shirley's Bonneville and head for home. But somewhere on the outskirts of Hermon, I think, Shirley gets a little mixed up. I'm not saying the Moose Juice we drank at lunch had anything to do with it, but somehow we got lost. However, as Caitlin says, "the universe works in mysterious ways." We rounded the corner, and there it was: Sweet Dreams Bakery.

"Stop! Stop!" we all yell. "Pull in here!" We just needed directions, you understand.

So we stroll into Sweet Dreams and the first thing that hits me is the smell, a chocolaty, brown-sugary smell. Then I see two glass-fronted cases just plumb-chuck-a full of sweets. Oh, my God, I'm thinking, where has this place been my whole life?

The fella behind the counter must have been joking when he asked, "Can I help you ladies?"

"Yes!" Shirley says. "We're lost and need some sugar to find our way home!"

Oh, there was some hard deliberating, as you can imagine, but finally, we ordered. Celeste chose a double chocolate brownie with peppermint frosting. Rita picked a Death-by-Chocolate flourless torte. Betty had a lemon tart with shortbread crust, and Dot the Mixed Berry Crumble a la Mode. Shirley went for a Chocolate Volcano (I almost ordered that, too), which was this chocolate cake with a liquidy chocolate center, served with a raspberry sauce. (I know! I can't for the life of me remember what L-glutamine does, but I know what every single one of us ordered for dessert that day. It's crazy!)

Everyone loved their choice, but mine was positively erotic—a chocolate-cookie crust filled with homemade caramel, drizzled with chocolate sauce, and then, wait for it, a generous sprinkling of Maine sea salt. I get weak-kneed just thinking about it! That dessert was the perfect blend of sweet and salty, a combination that's grown more and more appealing the older I get. Reenergized, we hopped into the Bonneville and cruised back to Mahoosuc Mills without a hitch.

I want you to know I'm still thinking about that dessert. The other morning at the breakfast table, Charlie caught me staring off into space.

"Ida," he asked, "you all right?"

"Oh, I'm fine," I says. "Just havin' myself a sweet little daydream, is all."

 Straight Talk from the Barcalounger: How I Look Out for Number One

R&R? Me in my Barcalounger with the remote control. Whether it's in the semi-reclining position or all the way back, that puppy works like a charm. I get home from the mill, pick up the remote, and settle in to watch the news. I forget about work and before I know it supper's ready.

Ida's not quite as fond of the remote or channel surfing as I am.

"Can we just settle on something, Charlie," she says. "It seems like we never watch a show all the way through. It's like the remote control's been surgically implanted into your hand."

And I'm thinking, "A man can dream, can't he?"

So last weekend, I was settled in for some major rest and relaxation when I hear Ida yelling at me. "Charlie, will you stop it? You're driving me crazy!"

"What? I'm watching the game."

"You are not."

"How do you know?"

"Well, the tip-off is the fact that you're snoring with such force I'm afraid you're gonna strip the paint off the walls. If you want to take a nap, go into the bedroom and close the door."

There are some things women will never understand.

Naps. Are. Good.

Another great way to nourish my inner spirit is napping. But with my day job down to the A&P, I'm kind of restricted to napping only on weekends. I've lobbied the A&P for years to put in an employee nap room, but no go. Can't understand it.

See, I'm a morning person. I wake up perky as all get out, just bursting with energy. Afternoons, however, are a different story, especially between the hours of three and four, which, as far as I'm concerned, is the toilet of the day. Sometimes I yawn so hard, I swear to God, it feels like I'm going to turn myself inside out. I get that "falling off a cliff" feeling, like my soul is leaving my body. But by napping, voila! I get two mornings in the day! It's a win-win situation.

I'm a firm believer in setting yourself up for success by looking for the win-win. It's so easy to see things as black and white, either-or. "Oh, I can't do that 'cause I'm busy with this." Cut yourself some slack! Next time you're thinking it's either going to be the New You Spa with the girls or Jimmy's Little League game, ask yourself: How can I change this from an either-or situation to a both-and?

This might mean (gasp!) asking for what you want! Call up the girls and see if they mind leaving for the New You at one instead of eleven so you can go to both the game and the spa. Or ask your dessert buddy if she wants to get the Chocolate Volcano while you order the Chocolate, Caramel, and Sea Salt Tart. Then the two of you can share. Oh, maybe I'll do that next time.

Dreaming of a Napping Gold Medal

If napping were an Olympic sport, oh mister man, I'd be captain of the team. Well, I've been in serious training most of my adult life. Which is weird, 'cause I was one of those kids who hated napping. I was so afraid of missing something, I'd fall asleep standing up. Now, I guess I'm making up for lost time.

Both Charlie and me are nappers, but we have different styles. Charlie's a sprinter; he reclines in his Barcalounger when he gets home from work and usually naps ten or fifteen minutes before supper—"putting his feet up," as he calls it. On the weekend, he'll nap big-time in the Barcalounger. His preferred napping technique is the fully clothed, flat-on-your-back luge position with slight variations, say, feet crossed, or uncrossed.

I am more of a long-distance napper. I prefer a freestyle napping technique, using the tuck position, right or left side, or the half tuck on stomach (again, right or left), with a pillow. (The judges may quibble, but I insist on using the pillow to support my upper tucked leg.) For maximum effect, I occasionally employ the horizontal pike position, but I'm a curler at heart.

As with any sporting activity, you get a better performance by wearing the proper gear. I prefer the "dress in what you wear to bed" napping attire.

196

Both wrapping a pillow around your head to drown out the snoring of your spouse and pillow-hugging are frowned upon in the couple's napping events, of course, with style points deducted from the overall score. Immediate disqualification occurs for any of the following violations of the Good Napping Code of Ethics: snorting, drooling, snoring so loud you wake yourself up, or waking up and not knowing what time it is, day it is, or what planet you're on.

> *A while back, I woke up from my nap, stretched, and pulled something in my neck. When I told Charlie about it, he goes, "Let me get this straight. You had a napping-related injury?"*

Like with any extreme sport, there is the danger of injury. A while back, I woke up from my nap, stretched, and pulled something in my neck. When I told Charlie about it, he goes, "Let me get this straight. You had a napping-related injury?"

But I didn't let my injury slow me down. No way! I got back into our bed on Sunday and sacked out for an hour. Yup, to excel at napping takes commitment. You may decide to specialize in one area of napping, or to be more of a generalist. The field's wide open. Charlie and me are currently considering the tag-team napping relay. Kind of ambitious, I know, but you only live once.

A Gratitude List

Sometimes setting yourself up for success means planning ahead. We're told to do this when we're dieting. You know, cook some meals ahead of time and freeze 'em. Have the dreaded baggie of carrot and celery sticks at the ready. Planning ahead works for nourishing your inner spirit, too. Schedule some reenergizing appointments with yourself, so they don't get lost in the shuffle. Put them on your calendar, if you have to. Set aside fifteen minutes when you get home from work to sit and have a cup of tea before you start supper. Or take an adult ed class in rug hooking, scrapbooking, or Crock-Pot Magic— whatever floats your boat.

> There's something about having your hair done together that's bonding. Did you see that movie, *Steel Magnolias*? It's kind of like that at the shop, only with snow and black-flies. We call ourselves the Sturdy Pinecones.

I love my weekly appointment down to Hair Affair with Patsy and the gang. The Saturday-morning crew don't really spend time together outside of Hair Affair (except for Estelle Fournier and Denise Ouellette, who are sisters). But still, we know quite a bit about each other 'cause there's something about having your hair done together that's bonding. Did you see that movie, *Steel Magnolias*? It's kind of like that at the shop, only with snow and blackflies. We call ourselves the Sturdy Pinecones.

Having a hobby is a great way to nourish your inner spirit. And having a craft room is the perfect place to take a little time out from your husband when he's driving you crazy.

As much as I try, sometimes reconnecting and reenergizing gets totally lost in the business of everyday life. Especially during the holidays. So, I always try to take January 2 off from work as a recharging day. I wake up with that wonderful feeling of starting fresh, like I used to get as a kid after going to confession at church. My goal for that day is to make a list of all the things I'm grateful for.

See, I keep a gratitude journal all year, just like Oprah. Every day I write down at least five things I'm grateful for. You know—like I'm grateful for how pretty that cardinal looked on the bird feeder this morning, or that I didn't have a second brownie at book club. But on January 2, I make a big list with as many things as I can think of. I work on it off and on all day. When I'm finished, I take that list, put it in an envelope, and write on the outside, "To be opened in case of an emergency. Love, Ida."

Then I go into my craft room and tack it up on my bulletin board in place of last year's list. I always read last year's list to see how I'm doing on the gratitude front, making sure I didn't forgot anything on my new list, before retiring the old one to my gratitude file. I have lists going back about ten years, I think. That's a lot of gratitude. Just seeing that envelope on my bulletin board perks me up. It's comforting to know it's there. If I'm running low on gratitude, in need of a little reenergizing, I know I can go into the craft room, read my list, and top off the tank.

 Caitlin's New Age Nook: Aromatherapy
When it comes to self-care, aromatherapy is a wonderful tool. Different essential oils have unique properties that can be used to affect our mood. You can buy candles with these scents. We have some wonderfully fragrant soy candles at Mahoosuc Health Food. Or you can use a diffuser and an essential oil. There are different kinds of diffusers: steam, clay, or simple ones that work with water and a tea candle.

Two great scents to start off with are peppermint and lavender. Peppermint will reenergize you, perk up your mood, and clear your head. It's clean and refreshing. Lavender is a more mellow fragrance. It's a stress reliever, good for recharging through deep relaxation. Keep both on hand for a quick, easy, and inexpensive way to pamper yourself.

 Aunt Ida Tweaks It
Like I said before, smells really affect me, so I'm all over this one. Say I'm at work. It's three-thirty in the afternoon, and I'm hankering for a nap, having a hard time concentrating. I can't exactly whip out a peppermint candle and start meditating at Register 3. But, I can have a York Peppermint Patty, making sure to sniff at that peppermint filling between bites. Even a breath mint or a piece of peppermint gum will do the trick, reenergizing me enough to make it through 'til five.

As a stress reliever, I always keep some lavender hand lotion in my pocketbook. I also have these nice little lavender sachets that Caitlin gave me for my birthday. I keep those in my lingerie drawer so I know that deep down, I'm stress-free. And nothing says relaxation like a long, hot bath with some lavender bath salts.

B-Positive

One of the best ways I know to nourish my inner spirit is to give back. You don't have to write some big check to a charity, but you could buy some Girl Scout cookies or put a dollar in the Salvation Army bucket. You can volunteer on a weekly basis or for a special event. Or bake some brownies and take 'em down to the Senior Center. Ask if you can do anything that day to help them out, or just drop off the brownies knowing you've made some elderly folks happy. Sometimes the littlest thing can make a difference in someone's life. And if you're in a funk, putting the focus on someone else helps you get over it and reconnect with yourself.

I remember a month or so after my mom died, as we were approaching our first holiday season without her, Dad, Irene and me were feeling blue. So as a family, we volunteered down to St. Hyacinths'—putting together food baskets and delivering them to needy families. It's the best thing we could've done. We felt useful and grateful for our blessings. We started focusing on what we had, not on what we'd lost. By reconnecting and reenergizing, we could face the holiday—if not with enthusiasm, at least without dread.

You could also give blood. It's one of them real feel-good things to do. My dad's done it for years, so you'd think I'd have followed suit. But somehow, I just never have. I'm not afraid of needles or nothing; it just never quite made it to the front burner.

But a while back, I saw this story on television about a man who had donated blood his whole life, as often as he could. He was a real geezer now, but over the years, they figured he'd donated gallons and gallons of blood. Imagine!

Well, that story really stuck with me. So when I saw that the Red Cross was holding a blood drive down to the Kiwanis Club, I decided the time had come. Heck, I thought, why not get the Women Who Run with the Moose to join me? As I told 'em, here's a way we can help people that won't cost us a penny. It only takes about an hour, and I hear snacks are involved.

> They give us first-time blood donors a big green sticker. Didn't go with my blouse, but I let it slide.

Rita was the only reluctant one. She tends to be a little squeamish, but we shamed her into it. Turns out Shirley's given blood before. She's O-positive, which

I guess is the blood type the Red Cross wants most. They were pretty darn pleased to see her.

"What type are you, Ida?" Shirley asks me.

"B-positive."

"Figures," she says, rolling her eyes.

Well, didn't they have the setup down to Kiwanis! It looked kind of like *M*A*S*H*, only nicer. There's a bunch a stuff you have to read before they sign you up. I breezed through that. They give us first-time blood donors a big green sticker. Didn't go with my blouse, but I let it slide.

Then this nurse takes me to a little cubicle and starts asking me questions, and then I had to answer even more questions on the computer. I remember this was why my dad quit giving blood: the darn questions. They were all about living outside the country and having sex with prostitutes and gay men. Dad was seventy-eight years old at the time, and there just wasn't much of that kind of thing going on down to Mahoosuc Green. That said, if me or someone I cared about had to have a blood transfusion, I'd be mighty glad these questions were asked.

Well, they tested my iron level, took my blood pressure and pulse, and all systems were go. "My veins aren't the best," I told Nurse Mary as I hopped up on the table. "Last time I had a colonoscopy, it took 'em three tries to get the IV going."

"Not to worry," Mary says. "I've been doing this for years. Should be no problem." She paints my arm with iodine, finds a good vein, and puts the needle in. Nothing. A little blood in the bag, then it stops. I felt bad for Mary. She knew it was my first time, and she was kind of upset, I could tell. Her supervisor, Linda, came over, and they fiddled with the needle for a bit, but no go.

202

"Want to try the other arm?" I ask. No, they explained. They couldn't. Once they get some blood in the bag, that's it.

"You've got to be kiddin'," I says. I was so disappointed. "Is it because I got low blood pressure or something?"

Linda told Mary to take a little lunch break. After Mary was out of earshot, Linda told me they can only feel the vein, they can't really see it. So Mary must've nicked it a little going in, causing a bruise, and when that happens, the blood stops flowing.

> *"A bruise?" I ask, my mind racing ahead to a potential fashion quandary.*

"A bruise?" I ask, my mind racing ahead to a potential fashion quandary.

"Won't last," Linda assured me, as she put a Band-Aid on me and applied some ice. "Six weeks, and you'll be good as new," she kidded. "No, really, ten days to two weeks tops."

What kind of field trip is this, I'm thinking, as I wander over to the snack table to self-medicate with some Cheez-Its and a couple of Oreos. The rest of the girls were still on the tables, chatting away and giggling. Seeing as it was so nice out, I told them I'd wait outside.

Celeste, Rita, Betty, Dot, and Shirley were in fine spirits when they emerged from Kiwanis. They'd done their good deed and were all hopped up on sugar.

Rita goes, "That was easy. I think we should do this every couple of months." And everyone agrees.

Then Shirley goes, "Gee, Ida, what's up? You look a little B-negative."

I explained what had happened—how I got defective veins and all, and they tut-tutted and marched me off to the Busy Bee for a late breakfast. When I saw that side of bacon, I knew it wasn't the end of the world.

Dream a Little Dream

When you take care of yourself, you're able to show up in your life and live with integrity. That means not only being upright and honest with others, but honoring yourself, too, and protecting what's important.

Besides family, the most precious things we have—in my opinion, the things most in need of protection—are our time and energy and our dreams and ideas.

Listen, we only have a limited amount of time in this life, and as my friend Betty, who's a golfer, says, "I'm on the back nine." In other words, I've lived more of my life than I have left. To be honest, I just don't have as much get-up-and-go as I used to. When I think about it like that, why in God's name would I choose to squander my precious time and energy doing something out of a misplaced sense of obligation? The world does not revolve around me, and it will not come to a screeching halt if I don't go to a Tupperware party given by the cousin of a friend! Am I right?

Next. Have you ever had a dream to do or make something, or an idea that made your heart sing? My feeling is, if it makes you happy and it's legal, go for it! But have you ever shared that dream or idea with a so-called "friend," and they pooh-poohed it, tried to talk you out of it, or downright stomped on it? (Listen up, Claudia Peavey!) Then there's the "considerate" person who nicely tells you they're just trying to be realistic, you know, "for your own good." Well, folks, that's their reality. It don't have to be yours!

You wouldn't leave your children with someone who was unable to protect them, would you? So why would you entrust something as fragile and precious as a dream or an idea to someone who, you know in your heart, won't get it, doesn't believe you deserve it, or is just plain jealous of you and your good idea? And why are you wasting time and energy on "friends" like that in the first place?

The Dog Poop Dilemma

Treating yourself with integrity means being true to yourself whether someone's watching or not. For example, when I'm walking our little dog, Scamp, and he stops to poop in the deserted corner lot over on Depot Road, it would be easy to just let it be. But I pick up the poop regardless. It's a commitment I've made to myself. I thought Charlie and me were on the same page with this one, but was I ever in for a rude awakening.

Like I said earlier, Charlie usually takes Scamp out for his morning constitutional, and I do the afternoon walk. But one Saturday afternoon a while back, we were both hanging around the house, and I thought, Wouldn't it be nice to take a little walk together?

It starts out pretty much ho-hum. We're walkin' and talkin' about nothing much, like you do. When Scamp stops to do his business, like dog owners everywhere, we stop talkin' and watch. So I get out a plastic bag to pick it up, you know, to be a good citizen, and Charlie says, get this, he says, "Ida, don't bother."

"Huh?"

"It's not big enough to bother with."

Well, that brought me up short. "Are you telling me there's a minimum size for scooping poop?"

"Yeah," he says.

205

I bagged Scamp's deposit anyway, and we continued on our way.

"So, let me get this straight," I say. "There's some kind of system for determining if a poop is big enough to pick up?"

"Well . . ."

"You bring a ruler or something? Do you have one of them gauge things, like for lobsters, that you pull out and go, 'Yup, that's a keeper?' "

"No, you don't need a ruler."

"Then how do you know?"

"I just know."

Charlie and me walked in silence for a bit, me pondering this information. I wasn't buying it.

"Well, then," I says, "what about on your morning walks when Scamp does his business twice? Do you bring two bags or one, and go in for the double scoop?" (Personally, I go for the double scoop. I know it's an advanced maneuver, but I have special skills from working checkout down to the A&P. It's all in the wrist.)

"One bag," Charlie replies. "And after the first scoop, that's it. Tie 'er up and call it a day."

"And the second time?"

"The second time is just an afterthought. Not enough to bother with."

"You just leave it?"

"Yup. But I take a stick and kind of disperse it."

"Disperse it?"

"Yeah, you know, kind of blend it in with the surroundings."

"So, you bring a stick on your walk?

"No, I just find one."

"Charlie," I reason. "Wouldn't it take less time to just pick up the poop?"

"Maybe, but I left the bag back at the first spot, to retrieve on our way home."

"So that's when you reach for your second bag."

"Don't need a second bag, Ida. It's not big enough to bother with."

After forty years of marriage, you think you know someone. Then something like this comes up, and you find yourself thinking, Who is this guy?

The Express Lane of Life

It's interesting to me how hard people work to justify their behavior. Like Charlie does with his minimum-size poop, or people in the express lane down to the A&P. I've been working there since I was seventeen, and believe me, I've seen it all.

In my opinion, how people act in a grocery store is a good indication of their personal integrity. For example, let's say we got a pyramid of pink grapefruit over in produce and somebody takes one from the middle, and the whole pile of grapefruit starts to spill on the floor. Does that person walk away, pretending they had nothing to do with the spill? Do they report it and let someone else deal with it? Or do they try to put it to rights? Does a bystander seeing this whole thing move on, not wanting to get involved? Or does the bystander give the culprit a dirty look and report them? Do they pitch in and help? You get the idea.

They say "The eyes are the mirror of the soul," but I got to tell you, from the cashier's point of view, there's no better place to size up someone's personality than the express lane.

> *In my opinion, if the IRS wants to know who's probably cheating on their taxes, all they have to do is hang around the express lane. 'Nuff said!*

"Fourteen items or less" to most people means just that. It's a courtesy to the rest of our shoppers. You got more items than that, you line up with the shopping-cart people, okay? I knew Caitlin's boyfriend Adam was a keeper when I saw him counting the stuff in his basket, shake his head, and move over to a regular register. (This was before he knew I was her aunt, so he wasn't doing it just to impress me.)

There are special circumstances, of course. You know, there's a long line at all the other registers, and you have more than fourteen items and you're in a hurry, so you stand in the express lane, sweating a little, feeling guilty. But you need to get home to cook dinner and get Becky off to band practice. Who hasn't been there? Long as this doesn't happen every week, I'm willing to let it slide.

But how about those chronic offenders? Folks who read "Fourteen items or less" as "Fourteen kinds of items or less." We've all been behind these guys. In their heads, they're counting twelve yogurts as one item. So there's the twelve yogurts, two half-gallons of milk, six Lean Cuisine frozen dinners, four cans of cat food, three one-liter bottles of diet root beer, and nine other items, which somehow adds up to fourteen.

In my opinion, if the IRS wants to know who's probably cheating on their taxes, all they have to do is hang around the express lane. 'Nuf said!

Blood Oath

I learned about integrity early on by observing life in Mahoosuc Mills. Back then, people made deals with a hand-shake. You gave your word, and that was good enough. Some folks still do business that way. See, when you live in a small town, it's important to protect your reputation 'cause people have long memories.

Grampy Gilbert taught me the value of giving my word when I was a young whip-persnapper. I was reminded of this last spring when I was straightening out our storage shed, and I come upon his old fishing creel. Beautiful thing.

> *"I, Ida Gilbert, swear to never tell anyone where Grampy's secret fishing spots are." I printed my name with a back-wards "d," "Iba." Heck, I was only five!*

I opened the lid, and inside was a blood oath he made me sign as a kid. I promised to never tell anyone where we'd gone fishing. Those spots were secret!

Since Grampy was basically illiterate, I think my grand-mother must've wrote the oath out for him. On the first day I went fishing with him, sitting in his truck in our driveway, he had me sign it: "I, Ida Gilbert, swear to never tell anyone where Grampy's secret fishing spots are." I printed my name with a backwards "d," "Iba." Heck, I was only five! Then Grampy heated a straight pin with his lighter (honest to God), gave my finger a little poke, and had me put my fingerprint in blood beside my name. He tucked that piece of paper into the pocket of his plaid shirt, and off we went. At the start of every fishing season, he'd have me renew my vow by putting my hand over my heart and repeating that oath.

Grampy gave me that fishing creel a couple years before he died. He was having trouble getting around on his own, and knew he wouldn't be needing it. He made me swear my oath again, for good measure, and tucked that piece of paper inside. That's where it's been ever since.

I never did tell anyone about those fishing holes (except Charlie, of course—but he's family, so it doesn't count). I hadn't thought anything of it until last spring. When I found that blood oath, I realized something I hadn't before, something Grampy knew all along; that oath wasn't with him, it was with myself.

So, instead of putting my blood oath back in the fishing creel, I brought that faded piece of paper into the house and I placed it in my gratitude journal. It's a daily reminder to keep my word, not only to others, but to myself, too.

Gettin' Going

- Make a date with yourself to do something that nourishes your inner spirit. Put it on your calendar. Try doing this once a week for a month.
- Look for the win-win. The next time you're thinking it's either this or that, stop, and ask yourself, "How can I change this from an either-or situation to a both-and?"
- Keep a daily gratitude journal. Think of one thing you're grateful for when you get into bed at night. Or start a big gratitude list and keep it where you can see it, in case of a gratitude emergency.
- Buy some lavender hand lotion, a scented candle, or bring in the big guns and get a diffuser and some essential oils.
- Volunteer, give blood, write a check—whatever you can do to give back.

- Ask yourself, "Will the world come to an end if I'm not there?" the next time you find yourself thinking, "I don't really want to go to something or other, but I feel obligated."
- Stop wasting energy trying to justify something, whether to others or to yourself. If you find yourself doing this, try another course of action.

Eleven

Girls Just Wanna Have Fun!

Wait a minute! Did I just sense you thinking, "Geez, it's been so long since I've really had fun, I don't know what it is anymore?" Not to worry. It's like riding a bike, which, after all, you loved doing when you were a kid, and just might love again.

When it comes to livin' the good life, you can't underestimate the importance of fun. Follow-your-bliss fun, take-a-mental-health-day-from-work fun—good-silly fun. Adding more fun into your life will make you happier and healthier, so you'll look and feel younger. When you're having more fun, the people around you tend to have more fun, too, which will make your relationships with family, friends, and coworkers that much better. Plus, fun reenergizes and recharges your inner spirit. Fun is the secret ingredient that makes it all work.

Fun is different things to different people. You just need to find what works for you. For example, the mere thought of keeping one of them little bonsai trees alive sounds about as much fun to me as swatting blackflies. To someone else, it could be as relaxing as taking a nice hot bath. Doing crafts may not appeal to you, but put a hot glue gun in my hand, and

> *I believe that if I'm real bad in this life, when I die, I'll be sent someplace where I have to play board games all day. It'll just be me and the devil playing Monopoly, over and over and over for eternity.*

I'm as content as a kid with a Creamsicle. Don't ask me to play a board game, though. I don't get the fascination with them. I believe that if I'm real bad in this life, when I die, I'll be sent someplace where I have to play board games all day. It'll just be me and the devil playing Monopoly, over and over and over for eternity.

Going Stealth

While doing our research, Caitlin read that moose can run twenty miles an hour for several miles at a time. I didn't believe it. But then, just this last spring, Dot and Tommy were driving up to their camp. It's a dirt road, full of tricky curves, and 'round one of them curves they come upon a moose. That critter takes one long look at Dot and Tommy's truck approaching, then bolts down the road in front of 'em, kind of leading the way, for six and a half miles! I asked Tommy how fast they were going. "I couldn't believe it," he says. "The darn thing was clippin' along at eighteen, twenty miles an hour the whole time!"

So, as it turns out, not only are moose good swimmers, they're long-distance runners, to boot! You'd think you'd be able to hear a beast like that a mile away, but they're amazingly quiet. Plus, they have this uncanny ability to blend in with their surroundings.

One time, Charlie was out hunting partridge in the woods, when he thinks he sees something out of the corner of his eye. He stops and gets real quiet, slowly turning his head in that direction. Nothing! He's staring into the woods for a good thirty

214

seconds or so, the way he tells it, then things come into focus. Suddenly, he realizes that there's this big bull moose, not more than ten feet away, staring right back at him. Charlie says he just stood there, frozen, for I don't know how long. Finally, the moose let out a snort and sauntered off. Charlie was so shook up, he called it quits for the day.

Moose have a way of moving with speed and grace, all the while flying under the radar. Kind of like middle-aged women, am I right? Sure, we're invisible to most folks, but it's amazing what we can accomplish when they don't see us coming!

Celeste, Rita, Betty, Dot, Shirley, and me call it "going stealth." It probably won't help you get a Grande Mocha Café Latte at Starbucks, but it does free you up to try new things.

Women Who Zumba

A while back, us girls started taking a Zumba class given by adult ed down to Moose Megantic High. You've heard of Zumba, right? It's this Latin dance/exercise thing. It was Betty's idea, of course. She's always up on the latest stuff. "Zumba's supposed to be wicked fun," she says. "Kind of like *Dancing With the Stars*, only without the skimpy outfits."

And without the cute guys, I'm thinking. 'Cause you can bet it's only going to be middle-aged women at this thing, wearing sweatpants and big T-shirts.

That first night, there was this twitter of excitement when a nice-looking young fella walks into the gym. But turns out he was just looking for the class in small engine repair.

Celeste whispers, "Wish I was a small engine . . . "

"Vroom, vroom!" Shirley replies.

215

"Okay, class!" shouts Monica, our teacher, this little wisp of a thing who's probably half the age of anybody in the room. "Is everyone ready to Zumba?"

"Yes!" we yell, a tad tentatively.

Boom!

Boom!

Boom!

This Latin-y kind of music kicks in, and we're off.

Halfway through class, I look over at Dot who's hanging on for dear life. "Jeezum crow!" she says. "I took Latin in high school. I thought this would be easy!"

"Tell me about it, Dottie! No wonder they call it the 'hottest exercise craze.' I'm sweating buckets!"

But listen, once you get the hang of it, Zumba's wicked fun. I always stand in the front of the class so I can see the teacher better. Helps me pay attention.

Here's the deal, though: We're not always facing front. With Zumba, not only is there a lot of cha-cha-ing and shimmying (I just love to shimmy!), there's a fair amount of pivoting, too. And when we pivot, I end up in the back of the room. (Kind of like Caitlin's perspective exercise, right? All of sudden, I'm looking at things from a different angle.) And it always makes me smile. As I turn, here's what I see: fifteen or twenty middle-aged women not caring what anyone thinks, shaking it and feeling it, "livin' la vida loca!" And they're just beautiful. Every single one of 'em!

> *Here's what I see: fifteen or twenty middle-aged women not caring what anyone thinks, shaking it and feeling it, "livin' la vida loca!" And they're just beautiful. Every single one of 'em!*

216

Afterwards I says to the girls, "We need to take this Zumba feeling out of the classroom and into real life. No one's paying attention to us anyway, so why are we worrying what people think?"

They all agreed. Even Shirley, who, I've got to say, looks more like she's Irish step-dancing during class than doing Zumba. Shirley goes, "I still don't think some of those moves are legal in Maine! But it was worth it to see Claudia Peavey smile. I didn't think she had it in her."

How to Zoom-Zoom

Now, whenever we're out and about as a group and one of us girls is acting small in the world (you know what I mean), the rest of us will go, "Zoom, zoom. Zoom, zoom!" That has a way of snapping her out of it.

When I'm all by my lonesome, though, I have to "zoom-zoom" myself, if you know what I'm saying. For me, it works best if I stop, put my hands on my heart, and say, "Zoom, zoom." Then, if no one's around, I cha-cha right, cha-cha left, shimmy right, left, and do it again. Then I take a deep breath in, sigh it out, close my eyes for a sec, and I'm good to go.

So, if you find yourself acting small in the world, needing a little pick-me-up, just go, "Zoom, zoom!" If you're shy, and people are around, do what I do: cha-cha and shimmy in your head. Or, you can go to the restroom and do it!

"Zoom, zoom" really works for me. It helps me feel my feet on the ground, and focuses my attention back where it belongs, not on what others might think.

Caitlin's New Age Nook:
How Big Is Your Slice of Fun?

Do you need more fun in your life? Here's an easy way to find out:

Take a piece of paper and draw a big circle. Then, divide that circle into pie pieces, each representing how much time you spend during the week doing the things you do (i.e., work, cleaning, meal planning, grocery shopping, cooking, laundry, child care, self-care, and fun). The size of the pie piece should reflect about how much time you spend doing each task. For example, if you spend the majority of the week at your job, work should be the biggest piece of pie.

Is the fun piece of your pie just too darn small? If your answer is "yes," it's time to put more fun in your life! A good way to start is by delegating chores that can be done by others. Maybe your children are old enough to start doing their laundry? Can you hire a cleaning person? Who else in the family can do the grocery shopping? Becoming aware of the situation is the first step in being able to carve out a bigger piece of fun for yourself.

Aunt Ida Tweaks It

Okay, I think all you really need here are three categories: work, chores, and fun. You can add "nourishing your inner spirit" into your fun slice, but it shouldn't take up the entire piece. In my opinion, you can't underestimate the importance of having silly fun, hanging out (or lollygagging about), and having a guilty pleasure or two!

Whatever Starts Your Tractor

As you'd expect, Charlie's idea of fun is a little different from mine. Case in point, one of *the* big events of Charlie's year is the annual Antique Tractor and Engine Show up to Bouchard's Farm. You should see him that weekend. He's just like a kid, he's so jacked up.

The tractor show is the kind of event where fellas like my husband gather 'round and gawk at old machines that don't really do much besides sputter, cough, and shake a lot. Somehow that just fascinates 'em. Charlie loves shooting the breeze with these guys about their machines, and how far a drive they had to make to get to the show. Apparently, there's a whole antique tractor and engine show circuit. People come in their RVs for the weekend, their little putt-putts in tow. They set up in Bouchard's field, which is all laid out in "avenues" named

> *The tractor show is the kind of event where fellas like my husband gather 'round and gawk at old machines that don't really do much besides sputter, cough, and shake a lot. Somehow that just fascinates 'em.*

after tractor and engine manufacturers—"Bessemer Boulevard," "McCormick Road," and "John Deere Drive."

There's the tractor parades on Saturday and Sunday for anyone old enough to drive, of course, and lots of tractor-pull events. Anything from the kiddie division to the transfer sled-pull, where tractors pull these enormous cement blocks and drivers get judged on how far they can pull 'em. There's an antique division and one for the new, higher-powered tractors. What happens is a tractor pulls cement blocks until the weight puts too much strain on the engine and the tractor does a wheelie, which is apparently very exciting to the menfolk.

I don't see all that much of Charlie that weekend. He's having too much fun on his own. Oh, they do have a barn dance Saturday night. I go to that. But mostly, it's just fun for me to see how happy it makes my husband.

For Charlie, one of the highlights of last year's show was this guy selling antique tractor seats. Well, it wasn't so much the seats that got Charlie's attention. It was the sign over the fella's booth, which read, HOT IN SUMMER, COLD IN WINTER, HARD ALL YEAR 'ROUND. One heck of a sales pitch, huh?

Charlie was over the moon about this silicone tape he bought. It's supposed to be even better than duct tape (which is high praise indeed). Charlie was telling the guy how frayed the cord on his screw gun's gotten.

"And electrical tape don't work, right?" the guys asks.

"Not for long, nope."

"Your hands get all sticky, don't they?"

"Yeah, makes a wicked mess."

"This, my friend, is what you need."

The guy explains how indestructible his tape is, how it goes on, won't get all over your hands, and how it'll stay strong and flexible virtually forever. "Eight dollars for one roll, three for eighteen."

Not one to go hog wild, Charlie says, "I'll take a roll!"

"I thank you, sir!" the salesman says, pointing to a photo of a basset hound above his table. "And I want you to know, your eight dollars goes right into dog food for Buddy, here." Which, of course, gets the two of them going on about their dogs!

Hands down, though, Charlie's absolute favorite thing at last year's tractor show was the old shingle-making machine. To him, it was the bee's knees!

One guy mounts a block of cedar onto the machine, and the saw cuts these thin slivers off it. Then another guy feeds the end of the shake into a slot to trim it, and hands it to a third guy who stacks it all nice and neat, log-cabin style onto a pallet. I'd have walked right past the exhibit, but Charlie says he watched these guys for at least an hour.

I ask Charlie, "Why do you like the tractor show so much?," and he goes, "I don't know, Ida. You'll look down, and there'll be a kid sitting at his dad's feet, playing with a toy tractor. And you just know, when that kid's old enough, he'll be competing in the pedal-tractor pull. Then he'll move on to motorized tractors, and join the all-ages tractor parades 'round the fairgrounds. You look around and see teenage boys and girls riding together on their parents' tractors, and young fathers riding tractors with their kids and dogs. Older guys compete in the tractor pulls. Then you walk by a couple of really old duffers standing 'round a tractor, reminiscing about how good she ran . . ."

"Gee, Charlie, that's really sweet. The whole circle of life, right there at Bouchard's Tractor Show."

"Yeah! Plus, you know anything with an engine gives me a thrill."

"I sure do, mister man. Vroom, vroom!"

Just a Little Kiss

One of the things I admired most about Grampy Gilbert was how fun-loving he was. Being around him was a treat because he seemed to have a good time no matter what he was doing. Didn't take things too seriously. Grampy was good at his job, but what made him a popular guide was his ability to show people a good time.

He was also an inspiration to me because Grampy really and truly did not care what people thought of him. I aspire to that.

Oh, he was a character, with his French accent, a Pall Mall dangling from the corner of his mouth, and his beat-up, green fedora. I've seen pictures of Grampy back in his heyday, and boy, he was a looker: a little wild and woolly, perhaps, but he cleaned up nice!

And, let me tell you, he had some stories. Grampy might have been quiet fishing, but back and forth in his truck I heard tons of tales. Then there were the ones I caught out of the corner of my ear at a grown-ups' party. A lot of those I only understood when I was older. Here's my favorite:

"This big guy comes up from Pennsylvania to go hunting. He gets off the train, and I'm thinkin', How's this fella even gonna hike a mile? He was huffin' and puffin' just lugging his gear over to my truck.

"So the first night, we're staying in this cabin I know of. I cook us up some grub, and the guy eats like he hasn't seen food before, and washes it all down with a few cans of beer. Then, we head off to our bunks.

"Before my head hits the pillow, that fella falls asleep and starts snoring. I mean, sawing wood 'til the cows come home and beat the band!

" 'Hank!' I yell, 'Pipe down!' He'd sputter to a stop for a minute, you know, like an old jalopy. Then he'd crank it up again. 'Hank!' I yell again, but it was no use.

"Finally, I get up, walk over to him, and kiss him on the lips. He wakes up, I smile, and go back to bed.

"He doesn't sleep a wink the rest of the trip, but me, I sleep like a baby!"

Straight Talk from the Barcalounger: Can't Get Enough of It

There's not much you can do about work, but you can do somethin' about fun.

Sometimes, I'll hear Ida talkin' on the phone with one of her friends, and she'll say, "I'd love to, but I really need to clean the house this mornin'." I mean, come on! All that says to me is, "I don't really want to."

Listen, if Pat or Junior give me a holler to go four-wheelin' with 'em, I'm there. You won't hear me goin', "Can't—gotta mow the lawn." The lawn's gonna be there when I get home, right?

I say, if you get an opportunity to do somethin' fun, take it! Life's too short.

I'll Have Some Breakfast, Hold the Tops

In a small town, one of the most dependable sources of fun is the extended practical joke. I mean, these things can (and do) go on for years, passed down from generation to generation.

Now, we don't go in for the mean-spirited jokes here in Mahoosuc Mills, or anything where a person could get physically hurt. That sort of thing's too easy. There's no finesse involved. No, a good practical joke takes planning and creativity. It takes time and commitment. 'Cause you know if you pull a practical joke on someone, they're going to do the same to you. And then you'll have to get back at them. It's a bond that's outlasted many a marriage, and when done well can be satisfying, and almost exhilarating.

There are two rules for practical joking:

Neither the joker nor the jokee is supposed to acknowledge head-on that it's happening.

It ain't over 'til it's over.

Here's a classic that took place, oh, a good twenty-five years ago now, when Charlie and the boys (Bud, Smitty, Pat, Tommy, and Junior) went hunting down 'round Parsonsfield. This is something they do every November.

Now me and the girls know that "hunting" is just an excuse for the guys to get together, go to a cabin in the woods, eat lots of meat, drink beer, and play cards. For God's sake, they practically need a U-Haul for all their "supplies." So the Women Who Run with the Moose figure it's our duty, while the men are off doing their thing, to go to Portland and spend money just to even things out. We head south on the Turnpike. Back then, we'd get rooms at the Swiss Chalet for a couple of nights. Go shopping at the Maine Mall one day, Portland's Old Port the next. Get a jump on Christmas, you know. We always have a hell of a good time!

So that November, we get off at Exit 8 (as it was called back then. They've since redid the numbers, but you know what? We still call it Exit 8). Anyways, so we got off at Exit 8 like we normally do. We're all laughing and gabbing a mile a minute, and before we know it, Shirley gets in the wrong lane and we have to turn right instead of left. Fine, no problem. We'll just pull in someplace and change direction.

So as a hoot, Shirley turns into Mark's Showplace. Now for those of you who don't know, or are pretending you don't (and you know who you are), that was a big place, not there anymore, on the outskirts of Portland that had girlie shows and a topless donut shop. I kid you not! On the marquee it said, "This week: Pandora Peaks." Well, that got us giggling.

Celeste says, "Gee, it's wicked busy for this early in the morning."

"Yeah," I said. "The donuts must be exceptional."

Then Betty says, "Look at those trucks. They look kind of like Bud's and Charlie's."

"Betty," I says, sizing up the gun rack and the GO SOX bumper sticker on the Ford, "that don't look like Charlie's truck. That *is* Charlie's truck."

And Celeste says that the other truck looked pretty familiar, too. "Hunting? My ass!" she says.

"No wonder Smitty didn't want me to cook him breakfast this morning," Rita muttered. "He had his mind set on them 'donuts.' "

'Course, Dot wanted to march right in there and give Tommy a talking-to, but I say, "Dottie, you ever hear the saying, 'Don't get mad, get even'? Well, we're going to have some fun with this one, dear! Get moving, Shirley. We don't want them to see us."

Well, we did some major brainstorming that weekend. And truth be told, we probably spent more money than we usually do, but we left Portland with a plan. We swore an oath to each other that we wouldn't say nothing to our husbands about seeing them at the topless donut shop. Our goal was to get them to 'fess up of their own accord. It was going to be a waiting game to see who cracked first. Them or us.

The first thing us girls decided to do was to leave *Playgirl* magazines 'round the house where the boys could find them. Just to get their attention. This involved a field trip, of course. Half the fun's the planning.

So we pile into Shirley's Bonneville. We'd decided not to buy the magazines in town. Figured the fewer people in on the joke, the better. We went to Bangor. Made a whole day of it.

Had lunch. Did some shopping. Dot got the cutest pantsuit at the Fashion Bug.

Anyways, then we go to a 7-Eleven on the edge of town. We get out of the car, go into the store. There's a teenage boy behind the counter: purple hair, nose ring, baggy clothing. You know the look: not very attractive. I'm studying that nose ring hard, thinking, God, I hope he don't have allergies. So we're looking at him weird, and he's looking at us weird. I don't think he knew what to make of six middle-aged women buying *Playgirl* magazines, decaf coffee, and Ring Dings.

As we're leaving the store, I says to him, "Once you get past a certain age, this is 'bout as much fun as you can hope for, dear."

Well, the minute we got into the car, we zipped into those magazines. Honest to God! Shirley almost went off the road when we showed her the centerfold.

> *I was a teenager before I knew what a man looked like without his clothes on. It was just my sister Irene and me. No brothers. So, the only naked men I ever saw were pictures of statues in books. I spent most of my teen years thinking a man's you-know-what was shaped like a leaf.*

I don't know about you, but unless you're in love with a man, they look kind of funny naked. Come to think of it, even when you're in love with a man, they look funny naked. Us girls agreed that looking at nude pictures of men don't turn us on. Good for a laugh, though.

See, I was a teenager before I knew what a man looked like without his clothes on. It was just my sister Irene and me. No brothers. So, the only naked men I ever saw were pictures of statues in books. I spent most of my teen years thinking a man's you-know-what was shaped like a leaf.

Well, there weren't no leaves in *Playgirl*. Fella sporting a tool belt though. Pretty silly if you ask me. Grown man hanging 'round a construction site buck naked except for a tool belt, with a very big tape measure.

When I got home, I put that magazine on my nightstand, (opened up, like I'd been thinkin' of doin' a little home remodeling), my reading glasses on top.

That night Charlie and I were in the den watching the tube. A commercial come on, and Charlie gets up to go into the kitchen to get something to eat.

"Charlie, while you're up, can you get me my reading glasses? I think I left 'em on my nightstand. There's some recipes in the new *Redbook* I want to look at."

Charlie comes back a few minutes later with my reading glasses, a funny look on his face.

"Thanks, dear. Where's your snack?"

"Not hungry," he replies. Charlie never said a word about the *Playgirl*. Though for a spell, he was a little more attentive than usual. And he picked his socks up off the floor for a whole week.

The *Playgirl* thing was just laying the groundwork. Us girls didn't get into full swing with "Operation Donut Shop" until the beginning of December when we got together to do our craft project for Christmas. We do this every year. Betty usually comes up with what we're going to make. She's the artsy one. Sometimes it's wreaths, or decorated cookies, or centerpieces.

Well, that year, we decided to make Christmas decorations out of donuts. See, none of the boys had said a word about the *Playgirl* magazines, so we wanted to see if they could put two and two together.

Dot had some coupons, so we bought a whole mess of Dunkin' Donuts and set to work. We had a heck of a good time decorating donuts with little red and green plaid ribbons, making angels out of crullers (that's them long twisty donuts) by adding wings, a halo, and them little plastic eyes. (Truth be told, I think they looked more like moths.) Betty made a beautiful centerpiece by gluing together donut holes to form a miniature tree, then glazing the whole thing with sparkles. I don't know what Rita made. No one ever does. The poor thing is craft-impaired.

I don't think Charlie knew quite what to make of our new Christmas decorations. Especially that mistletoe with a few Dunkin' Munchkins hanging down.

Ever since seeing the boys' trucks at the donut shop, we'd been leading up to our New Year's Day brunch at Celeste and Bud's. It's something we do every year. But we were aiming to make this one special. The whole gang was going to be there: Celeste and Bud, Rita and Smitty, Betty and Pat, Dot and Tommy, Shirley and Junior, and me and Charlie.

Us girls had done a lot of cooking for the event. We'd spent hours and hours frying up donuts. Nothing but donuts. That's all we were serving. And we'd ordered these special aprons. I still have mine. It's a bib apron, the plastic kind that ties around your neck, with the body of a curvy woman wearing black lingerie on it, and huge inflatable breasts. We're talking Dolly Parton big!

I wish you could have seen the boys faces when all six of us girls walked into the living room carrying trays of donuts, all wearing our special aprons.

"Donuts, boys?" It's a good thing it weren't summer, or they'd have been catching flies, their mouths were hanging open so.

Then, you could practically hear it as it clicked into place: Light dawns on Marblehead. Finally, the boys knew that we knew about the topless donut shop. They didn't know how we knew. But we knew they knew we knew.

There was a pregnant pause while they pondered the situation. Then Charlie says, cool as a cucumber, "Mmm-mmm, those donuts sure look good! I think I'll have me a chocolate sugared one."

"Here you go, dear. Made them myself."

"I bet you did. You been working overtime, haven't you, sweetheart?" he chuckles.

"You know me."

"Nice apron."

That was it. The party went back to normal. You'd think at least one of them men would have cracked and 'fessed up. Not a word. They just sat there, drinking coffee and eating donuts like they didn't have a care in the world.

Still, us girls took satisfaction in the fact that the boys knew we knew. God, did we laugh!

Valentine's Day that year started off pretty normal. Charlie gives me a box of Russell Stover assorted chocolates and a nice card. But then, as he's leaving for work, he tells me, real casual-like, to get dressed up that evening 'cause he's taking me down to Sky Lodge for dinner. I was a little surprised. That's more pricey than our usual haunts. But I figured, why not go with the flow, right?

So, that night I get all gussied up. I looked pretty darn sharp, if I do say so myself. Charlie, too. We get to the Sky Lodge, and the hostess, Georgiana, takes us to a big round table in the center of the room, and there's Celeste and Bud, Rita and Smitty,

Betty and Pat, and Dot and Tommy. Shirley and Junior arrived right on our heels.

I says to Charlie, "What are you boys up to?"

He looks at me just as innocent as a newborn lamb. "Nothing, dear. We just know how much you girls enjoy each other's company."

Well, we had a heck of a time that evening. The boys treated us like a million bucks. After dinner, we're sitting there waiting for coffee and dessert (they have a raspberry sour-cream pie at Sky Lodge that just about melts in your mouth), when the waitress, Margie, comes to our table with a tray. On it are six identical packages, small ones, wrapped in gold foil paper. She sets one down in front of each of us girls.

"Charlie, what's this?" I ask.

"Why don't you open it and find out?"

Normally, I carefully unwrap a package and save the paper, but I was so excited I just ripped the paper off, opened the box, and lifted up the tissue paper. And there, nestled inside, was a ticket to see the Chippendales at Mark's Showplace.

I look at Charlie, then at the girls, and the whole table bursts out laughing. Charlie puts his arm around me and kisses me on the cheek. "Charlie, I saw those Chippendales on *Oprah*. They're wicked good dancers or that's what I hear."

"Why don't you make a weekend out of it. Do a little shopping," Charlie said.

"Charlie, this is one Valentine's Day I won't soon forget dear. By the way, you know any good breakfast spots in Portland?," I said with a smile.

Fun in Mahoosuc Mills Is . . .

- Going with your husband to get a moose lottery ticket. (Qualifies as a date night.)
- Complaining about the snow, the heat, the mud, the black-flies, people from away—you name it!
- Taking bets on whether this will be the year Whitey Hebert chucks them moldy old blue tarps he uses to cover his permanent yard sale. Probably won't, but hope springs eternal.
- Watching town librarian Sadie Dupris bowl. Thanks to Sadie, Mahoosuc Mills has been one of the top three teams in the Franklin County Employees Bowling League for a couple of decades now. (Poor gal doesn't know her Dewey from her decimal, but darn, she's one heck of a bowler!)
- Bud's famous Baked Bean Breakfast Buffet: served down to the Busy Bee, Thanksgiving to New Year's. You can count on his holiday treat being (ahem) the gift that keeps on giving.

The Giant Pumpkin

You ever have that fleeting thought, Wouldn't it be fun to . . . or, That sounds like fun! I've always wanted to . . . but you never did anything about it?

You've heard the saying, "Follow your bliss," right? And if you're like me, your next thought is, Okay, sure, but what *is* my bliss? Some lucky people find their passion early on, but for most of us, it's trial and error. Who knows; you might never find it. But how will you know if you don't try? What have you got to lose?

The best way to illustrate this point is to tell you a story about our neighbor, Gretchen. Gretchen and her husband, Bill, moved down the street 'bout ten years ago, and we're mostly, "Hi! How you doing?" neighbors, with a "Nice day, huh?" occasionally thrown in for good measure.

Well, one day a couple of summers ago I'm walking Scamp around the block, and there's Gretchen, working in her yard. When I ask her how she's doing, she goes, "I'm growing a giant pumpkin."

"Excuse me?"

Gretchen was just bursting with enthusiasm. "I have some great female buds, and I'm trying to prevent just any old male from pollinating 'em."

Well, that got my attention. So Scamp and I mosey over to her garden patch, and sure enough, Gretchen's got a little bondage thing going in her garden. She's meticulously tied the big, yellowy-orange flowers on the pumpkin vine shut.

"I have some nice males on the vines out back. I got plastic cups over those, so they don't open 'til I'm ready for 'em!"

We went to check those out, too. Yup. There were plastic cups over these taller, bud-like things. "Tell me, Gretchen," I says, "is Bill helping you out, or is this just your project?"

"Oh, at first he was pretty blasé about it. He tilled a little plot for me, but that was the extent of it. Now that we're about ready to do the pollinating, though, he's on board."

"There you go," I says. "It's been my experience, that it's up to the wife to hold the greater vision for the couple."

"Ain't that the truth?" she says. "I never even thought of doing this before. Then, I was at my dentist, looking through the *National Geographic*, and they had this picture of a guy with his giant pumpkin. I mean, it was huge! And I thought, 'Huh! Growing a giant pumpkin. That sounds kind of fun!' "

"And here you are!" I says.

"Here I am! You want to be on my e-mail list? I'll send you updates."

"Sure!"

I got to tell you, Gretchen was just glowing. Radiant. Walking home with Scamp I thought, It's amazing what having a passion can do for your overall well-being. It doesn't matter what that passion is. Geez, it almost made me want to grow a giant pumpkin myself! Just kidding, of course, but Gretchen's follow-through was kind of inspiring.

A few days later, I get my first e-mail update. Talk about commitment. Gretchen and Bill had gotten up at five-thirty that morning to pollinate pumpkin flowers. Apparently, this involves taking the male bud-like things, removing their outer petals, opening up the female flowers and rubbing several male buds inside the female flower. Bill's photos made it look like there'd been some major partying going on, plastic cups strewn all over the yard!

Well, sure enough, two pumpkins started to form on Gretchen's vine. But apparently, if you want to grow a giant you have to make some hard decisions: only one pumpkin per vine. So Gretchen did what she had to do, and "Godzilla" was born.

I guess he started off kind of slow, but then Godzilla began growing by leaps and bounds, an average of ten pounds a day once it hit its stride. And the bigger it got, the fonder Gretchen grew of it. "Godzilla's bringing back all those motherly instincts of mine," she wrote.

To protect it from the sun, they stretched a blue tarp over it, and as the weather turned, they tucked it under a blanket at night to keep it from getting cold!

Laugh all you like, but that bugger topped out just shy of
three hundred pounds! People in town would drive by to gawk
at it. (Mahoosuc Mills hadn't seen that level of excitement in
years.) I'd be talking with Gretchen, and a car would slow
down, the folks inside all smiles and giving the thumbs-up.

Later that fall, Gretchen and Bill went to the Topsfield
Fair down there in Massachusetts, where every year they have
a Giant Pumpkin Contest. Alas, they left Godzilla behind.
Topsfield's serious business, I guess, and big as it was, their
beloved pumpkin wouldn't even qualify to enter.

I ran into them at the post office shortly after they got back.

"How was the fair?" I asked.

"Well," Gretchen goes, "they had some monstrous big pumpkins"—and here's where she winks at Bill—"but none were as
pretty as Godzilla!"

Okay, so what I love about this story is that Gretchen had a
thought: Growing a giant pumpkin sounds like fun. And instead
of letting it end there, or thinking, I could never do that, or,
Everyone will think it's a dumb idea, she followed through. She
got up off her duff and did it. Gretchen found her passion. And
passion is contagious. Pretty soon it was the buzz of the town.
It's that old ripple effect once again.

Girls Just Wanna Have Fun

When it comes to fun, it helps to have a theme song. It has
a way of getting you in a fun frame of mind. Do you know that
song, "Girls Just Wanna Have Fun," by Cyndi Lauper? I'd never
heard of it until a while back, when Celeste, Rita, Betty, Dot,
Shirley, and me were down to the Juggernaut Lounge at the
Holiday Inn.

It was Karaoke Night, and all the usual suspects were there. Henry Duquette (bless his heart) got up and sang the same song he does every week: "Pretty Woman." Alas, he's no Roy Orbison. 'Course, you could understand him better if he put his teeth in. Violet Hughes does a pretty decent job with "Crazy" by Patsy Cline. It always sounds so heartfelt because she has a crush on the bartender, Barney. But that's going nowhere, see, 'cause Barney's "not a ladies' man," if you know what I'm saying.

So anyways, us girls were gearing up for our big number: Reba McEntire's "I'm a Woman." It's a routine we put together back when we started doing country line dancing, you know, back in the early Paleozoic, and we haul it out every once in a while. It's our signature number, and a pretty darn good theme song.

We were getting ready to strut our stuff when this group of young gals from over to Dexter got up and sang "Girls Just Wanna Have Fun." And they nailed it! I mean, laughing and singing at the top of their voices. They owned that song! Celeste, Rita, Betty, Dot, Shirley, and me were so impressed we dubbed them honorary "Women Who Run with the Moose" for the night.

Later, when we piled into Shirley's Bonneville for the ride home, I says to the girls, "You know what? I got nothing against our theme song, but I think we should give theirs a try."

"Fine!" goes Betty. "You get a recording of it, and we'll learn it!"

I was going to buy that Cyndi Lauper CD the next time us girls went to Bangor, but Caitlin said she'd "download" the song for me and burn a CD. While she was at it, I had her make one for all the Women Who Run with the Moose. We may not be quite ready for the Juggernaut Lounge, but we play that song in the car whenever we go on a road trip.

Heck, I sing it in the shower!

Sometimes when Charlie's not home, I crank up "Girls Just Wanna Have Fun," and I blast my way through the housecleaning with a little singing and dancing thrown in for good measure. It's just such a perky number! Scamp doesn't know quite what to make of the whole thing, and usually trots off to hide in his crate. I don't take it personal. I'm too busy letting loose. Besides, what happens in the double-wide, stays in the double-wide.

Gettin' Going

- Look at the adult education brochure in your town and sign up for a class, maybe something you never thought about taking before. Some courses are just one night, so it may not be that big of a time commitment.
- Keep a notebook in your purse. Whenever you find yourself thinking, Gee, wouldn't it be fun to . . . or, That sounds like fun . . . write it down!
- Say to yourself, "I've always wanted to [blank]." Write down the first thing that comes into your mind. I don't care how silly it sounds. Write down another thing, and another. Keep doing this until you can't think of anything else. You can do it on and off for several days. I'll bet you'll be amazed how many things you come up with. Then, do one or more of the things.
- Make a list of three things you loved doing as a kid. Now think about how you can incorporate one into your life today. For example, we had a tire swing tied with a rope to the big oak tree in our front yard, and I used to love to swing. That got me to thinking about swinging with my grandmother in one of those bench swings out on her porch, something I hadn't thought about for years. And that led me

to getting a bench swing and putting it on our deck, where I just keep on swinging!

- Ask your spouse about what they truly enjoy doing, and why, and see if there isn't a way for you to find fun in it, too.
- Find a theme song. Play it in the car. Sing it in the shower. Put it on when you're alone in the house, and dance yourself silly.

Twelve

Livin' the Good Life

This is where I sum it all up. If you're in a big hurry you've probably just skipped to here anyway—you know, cut to the chase. (Not that I've ever done such a thing!)

Livin' the good life is different for everyone, but there are little things you can do that'll make your good life even better. The key is keeping an open mind and being willing to try new things. Remember—the only one who can make your life worth livin' is you.

The "Cap-up," as Grampy Gilbert Would Say

If you only get one thing out of this book, let it be the importance of having a positive attitude. I can't stress this enough. That and the ability to laugh at yourself will get you through many a pinch. In life, like most things, you get out of it what you put into it. If you want more positivity and laughter in your life, you have to put more positivity and laughter out into the world. Like my dad says, "Stay happy and enjoy where you're at."

It's easier to do this if you take care of yourself, of course. Things always look better if you're well fed and rested. Your body knows what to do; listen to it. Try to stop eating when you're satisfied. Look for ways to sneak exercise into your life as often as you can. And don't forget to breathe. Aim to age gracefully, which doesn't mean surrendering completely. It means accepting where you're at, and then doing the best you can with what you've got. You can't move forward if you're fighting being where you are. And don't forget to put yourself at the top of the list every once in a while. Treat yourself the way you'd treat a trusted friend, with love and respect.

And speaking of friends: They're important. Friends and family are the roots that keep you from toppling over at the slightest breeze. Tending to those roots is essential, which means spending quality time with those special people in your life. If you didn't win the lottery in the family department, cherry-pick a new one. And while you're at it, cut loose those energy vampires. Bottom line: Does spending time with someone make you feel drained or energized?

If you're married or in a relationship, make it a priority. Treat your partner with respect. Say please and thank you, and try to kiss each other hello and good-bye. And if your spouse is irritating the hell out of you, do something nice for him or her. Sounds wacky, but it works.

In terms of work, if you don't love it, aim for being neutral with it. Spending forty hours a week being resentful will spill over into the rest of your life, and that's not good. If you've got to be there, be there. Or look for a new job, one that plays to your strengths. Ask yourself, "What is my personal definition of success?," and act accordingly.

And when all else fails, clean house. This is the best way I know to get unstuck and help me look at things in a new way. I'm talking about not only decluttering your house, but decluttering your mind, letting go of worry, resentments, and regrets. Giving time away—volunteering—is also a great way to get the energy flowing.

My good life got better when I started paying attention: tuning in to my senses, and taking notice when things feel right or when they don't. Listening to that little voice in my head, and following through when it says things like, "Don't forget to take your cell phone off the charger and put it in your pocketbook," or "Give so-and-so a call," or "Look at the sale rack in the back of the store."

And remember, you have your own internal guidance system: your heart. Check in with it from time to time, make sure you're on the right track. Stop worrying about what people think, and don't forget to have fun!

The Good Life in Mahoosuc Mills Is . . .

* For more than a few seniors I know, bingo night down to the Community Center.
* Whitey Hebert finding something for free, then turning 'round and selling it to some poor sucker from away at his permanent yard sale.
* Our town center. (Yes, we have one. Don't blink as you're drivin' through, though, or you'll miss it.)
* Getting to the DQ before it closes and getting a Peanut Buster Parfait. Or snappin' up that last piece of peanut butter pie at the bean supper down to the Congo Church. Tastes better if you luck out like that!
* Hangin' out with folks you've known your whole life. That, to me, is "home."

Caitlin's New Age Nook: Visit Your Future Self

I saved my favorite visualization for last, but before I begin, I'd like to thank Aunt Ida for letting me share all my "woo-woo" ideas with you. Aunt Ida, you're part of my good life.

Now, here's the visualization. If you want the inside track on living your good life, the one that's right for you, talk to your future self. Really! Here's how. This exercise is best done with a friend. One person can read the instructions, while the other does the visualization, then vice versa.

You know the drill. Sit in a quiet place where you won't be disturbed. Become aware of your breath. Focus on your breathing, taking long, deep breaths in and out. Relax. Scan your body for any place you're holding tension. Breathe into that area, release, and relax.

Picture yourself going down a staircase. As you descend the stairs, you become more and more relaxed. At the bottom of the staircase, you will see a gate. Open the gate and enter.

You are now in your secret garden. It is filled with the scent of your favorite flowers, the sound of running water. Feel the warmth of the sun on your face, a gentle breeze. Hear the birds chirping. You see a gently winding path in front of you. Walk down the path.

As you come around the corner, you will see a small garden plot ready for planting. To the right of the plot is a stack of paper and a container with pens, pencils, crayons, and markers. Take a moment to think of all the things that have been holding you back, preventing you from living your good life. It could be an attitude that you've outgrown, a regret or resentment, a place or thing, a relationship. You are now ready to let these things go. Choose a writing implement and one by one, write the things you are ready to release onto a slip of paper, and throw it into the garden plot. Watch as it immediately composts into the soil. Keep writing and composting until you run out of things. To the left of the plot there are some garden implements. Till your composted soil, smelling the richness of the earth. When you've finished, take a moment to acknowledge all you've left behind here and give thanks.

When you are ready, continue on the path. Enjoy the freedom you feel now that you've lightened your load. The path continues to meander through the garden. Notice the richness of the colors; stop and smell a flower. After several turns in the path you come around the next bend and see a bench to the side of the path in a beautiful alcove. There is someone sitting on the bench. She turns to greet you, smiling. You recognize her immediately. It is your future self.

She is radiant. She embraces you, and a feeling of warmth and unconditional love envelops you. She invites you to sit down next to her. And you sit, in silence at first, just basking in her serenity. When and if you want, I invite you to ask your future self questions: Looking back at your life, what is the most important thing you'd like me to know? How do I get to the place of serenity and joy that you have right now? What is the key to my happiness? Talk until you're talked out. Or just sit and be with your future self. No pressure.

When it feels right, stand up and prepare to leave, knowing you can come back here at any time and be with your future self. Embrace the amazing person you are. Before you part, your future self hands you a bag filled with small, iridescent seeds. These are your hopes and dreams. Each seed glows from within, pulsating with energy and intention.

You return along the path the way you came, enjoying your newfound sense of calm and serenity. Notice the beauty around you, the sights, sounds, and smells. When you come to the garden plot you fertilized earlier, stop. Smell the richness of the soil. Become aware of the seeds you are holding. Feel their warmth as they radiate life.

Take the seeds from the bag and throw them into the garden plot. As you do, think of specific things you'd like to manifest in your life. Or just hold the intention of being open to your highest good. Or both. The bag is bottomless, so you can scatter as many seeds as you wish. Watch as the seeds immediately take root and spring to life, green shoots sprouting from the ground.

When you are ready, continue on the path, out of the garden and up the steps. Return to the room you are in now. Keeping your eyes closed, take a moment to absorb what you have experienced, to let it settle. Return to your breathing. Take three slow, deep breaths, and open your eyes.

 Aunt Ida Tweaks It

Remember that part when I said it's important to keep an open mind and be willing to try new things? Well, this is the kind of thing I was referring to. Caitlin's right. You need to rope a friend into doing this with you, one reading the exercise and the other visiting with their future self, then you can switch.

I did this with Caitlin and it was a mind-blowing experience. I admit I was a little nervous—and skeptical—at first.

I says to Caitlin, "Does anyone end up seeing their future self and she's a gnarly old hag with a bad attitude and poor personal hygiene? It'd be hard to recover from that kind of thing."

"Not to worry, Aunt Ida," she replies. "I've led this exercise many times, and no one has ever been disappointed. To a person, their future self is radiant, loving, and serene."

And you know what? She was right.

What Did We Learn from the Moose?

- Choose to be independent and good-natured. Remember, you are responsible for your own happiness, not everyone else's.

- To heck with being negative. Try focusing on the positive. Look for things to appreciate, and you'll find them. Smile, say hi, and tell someone they look good. Then watch for the ripples.

- Eat your fiber, leafy greens, and try to do some of the other stuff you know is good for you, because it takes more energy to avoid doing something than to actually do it. Oh, and if you find out what L-glutamine is for, please let me know.

- Protect what's important: your family, your time and energy, your dreams and ideas, and your friendships. Surround yourself with people who energize and support you, and do the same for them.

- Do what you do best, and if you're feeling stuck, clean house.

- Pay attention to your senses and trust what they tell you. Try looking at the whole picture, not just the surface.

- Take time to nourish yourself, to reconnect and reenergize. It's all about setting the stage for a win-win. Think, how can I change this from an either-or to a both-and. That way, you just might get more dessert!

- You were born with your eyes wide open. All you have to do is check in with your heart and remember what you were born knowing.
- Going stealth gives you great power. Own it! It's amazing what you can accomplish when they don't see you coming! And when you or someone you know is acting small in the world, "Zoom, zoom!"

Now, go out there and unloose your inner moose!

 Straight Talk from the Barcalounger: Keep It Simple

What does livin' the good life mean to me?

Well, to tell you the truth, it's really not all that complicated.

Kicking back in the Barcalounger with a Bud after a hard day's work while Ida cooks supper. Sitting in a canoe at sunrise with a fishing pole in hand. Seeing a moose after sitting quiet in the woods for hours, waiting. Living in Mahoosuc Mills, surrounded by good friends and married to my high school sweetheart.

The good life? I'm livin' it.

Epilogue

Saturday, I'm on my way home from my weekly appointment with Patsy down to Hair Affair, when on a whim, I turn into the Agway parking lot. Don't know why, 'cause I'd planned on going straight home to clean the house. It just kind of happened. Generally, Charlie's the one who shops at the Agway. Me, not so much. But there I was. So, I go inside thinking, Maybe I can find another hanging plant for the deck.

Well, no sooner do I get in the door, when who do I see? Debbie Plourde. I hadn't seen Debbie since Washington crossed the Delaware. She was a year behind me in school. Debbie left Mahoosuc Mills soon as she graduated, married a fella from Bangor who was in the service, and they've lived all sorts of places since then. She was home visiting her parents. Boy, did we have a nice little chat. Great to catch up!

So once we say good-bye, I'm heading for the hanging plants, when I see those great rubberized gloves for gardening. One season is about all garden gloves are good for, and mine were shot. So I snap up a pair of those, this great purple and pink petunia combo to hang over the deck, and the cutest garden gnome with his little donkey ('cause it was there and adorable).

I'm standing at the checkout, and this Badger Sleep Balm caught my eye. It has a sweet picture of a badger sleeping on the lid. Joyce Wilson—it's her family that owns the Agway—was running the register. She said the stuff is a marvel. You rub it on your temples, wrists, and lips when getting into bed, and it's real relaxing. Plus, it smells good.

"Joyce," I says, "can this stuff do anything about Charlie's snoring?"

Good salesperson that she is, Joyce replies, "Can't hurt to try!"

On my way out of the store, I got to thinking of my Grampy Gilbert. More than once I remember him telling me, "*Mon p'tit chou*, I learn early on, it's good to have a plan, but don't be stubborn about it, eh? Keep your eyes open for 'happy accidents.'

"Me? I decide to leave Quebec when I'm a young chipper. You know, find me a better life *dans les États-Unis*. My plan? Go to Woonsocket, work in the mill like my brother, Henri. But I get to Maine and decide to visit my cousin Ralph here in Mahoosuc Mills. And one night, at a dance, who do I see from across the room? Your grandmother. *Mon Dieu*, my heart skips a beat. So, I work up my courage and ask her to dance. Sweet thing, she takes pity on me. When I take her in my arms, *c'est ça*, eh? We just fit. Right then, my big plan flew out the window. Your *mémé* was the happy accident that changed my life."

Back in the Agway parking lot, I'm smiling as I put my happy accidents into the trunk of my car. Just then I hear a voice behind me. "Fancy meeting you here."

I turn 'round and it's my sister, Irene. "Reeny! How you doing?"

"Great! I was on my way back from the A&P and remembered I needed some potting soil."

"Hey," I says to her, "you want to catch a late breakfast down to the Busy Bee?"

"Sure, I could eat something. Let me get a bag of dirt and let's do it."

Irene got some of that Badger Sleep Balm too, which we're both loving. Got to tell you, though, it don't do squat for Charlie's snoring.

Oh, we had a great time down to the Busy Bee. I won't go into details. Let's just say bacon was involved. The whole morning ended up being a lot more fun than the one I'd planned for myself. I'm sure glad I stopped at the Agway when the notion struck.

It's always good to be reminded: Live your life on purpose, but stay open to happy accidents.

That's it for now. Catch you on the flip side!

About the Author

Writer and performer Susan Poulin is the author of ten plays, five of which feature her alterego, Ida LeClair. The first of these, 1997's Ida: *Woman Who Runs with the Moose!* was awarded the Seacoast Media Group's Spotlight on the Arts Award for Best Play and Best Actress. Moose was followed in 2005 by *Ida's Havin' a Yard Sale!*, for which Susan received SMG's Best Original Script and Best Actress award, and *A Very Ida Christmas* in 2008 (nominated for SMG's Best Original Script). The fourth installment in the series is *The Moose in Me, The Moose in You!* (2010), a motivational speech Ida gives as a Certified Maine Life Guide. Her newest Ida show is 2012's *I Married an Alien!* Susan also writes the popular Maine humor blog and podcast, *Just Ask Ida* (justaskida.com).

Since her debut, Ida has entertained thousands of people from Maine to Minneapolis with her unique brand of wit and wisdom. Her sense of humor simply knows no bounds. In fact, 2010 marked Ida's international debut. *Ida: Woman Who Runs with the Moose!* was produced by Tantramar Theatre in Amherst, Nova Scotia, featuring a Canadian Ida.

Selected by *Portland* magazine as one of the "Ten Most Intriguing People in Maine," Susan Poulin has been creating and touring her original theatrical productions since 1992. A graduate of the University of Southern Maine, she was a featured performer in *The Mirth of Venus* and *The Mirth Canal* at the Institute of Contemporary Art in Boston, and at The Maine Festival, the Minneapolis Fringe Theater Festival, and Portland, Maine's Cassandra Project. Her work has been supported by the New Hampshire State Council on the Arts, the Maine Arts Commission, and the Maine Humanities Council. Susan is also a

251

popular keynote speaker, and has brought her humor and insight to presentations for Seacoast Women's Week, the American Cancer Society (New England Division), and the Personal Historians National Conference. Her essays have been heard on both Maine and New Hampshire Public Radio.

Born in Jackman, Maine, Susan now lives in Eliot with her husband and collaborator, Gordon Carlisle, and their dog, Charlie (who oddly bears a striking resemblance to Ida's dog, Scamp).

About Ida

Ida LeClair lives in Mahoosuc Mills, a small town in western Maine, with her husband, Charlie, and their little dog, Scamp. When Ida's not busy telling you about the funnier side of life, she works as a cashier down to Super Food World (formerly the A&P), and moonlights doing books for Smitty's Hardware and the Mahoosuc Mills Mainely Maine store. Though her hobbies include Zumba, crafts, and country line dancing,

perhaps her favorite are the adventures she has with her friends, Celeste, Rita, Betty, Dot and Shirley (aka, the Women Who Run with the Moose). As a consummate yard saler, Ida is featured in *Bruce Littlefield's Garage Sale America*, and even delves into the realm of motivational speaking with her presentation, *The Moose in Me, The Moose in You!* For your weekly chuckle, check out Ida's popular Maine humor blog and podcast, *Just Ask Ida* (justaskida.com).

Acknowledgments

I'd like to begin by thanking Womenaid of Greater Portsmouth for asking me to present the 2010 keynote speech kicking off Seacoast Women's Week, and for going along with the idea of me delivering the speech as Ida. That keynote, *The Moose in Me, The Moose in You,* became a full-length play, which premiered at ACT ONE's Festival of Fun in 2010, and serves as the basis for this book. Thanks as well goes to ACT ONE's Stephanie Nugent, for your continuing support and belief in my work.

As Ida says, "The Internet is a wondrous thing," and that it is. I found several websites helpful in collecting facts about the moose and moose totem. These include mooseworld.com, nhptv.org/natureworks, drnikki.com, shamanicjourney.com, animaltotem.com, and spritualbutterflies.com. Information regarding "Fly Rod" Crosby came from the book, *Fly Rod Crosby: The Woman Who Marketed Maine*, by Julia A. Hunter and Earle G. Shettleworth Jr., as well as maineguides.com and findagrave.com. Thanks to all these sources for being there when I needed them.

Thanks also goes to Carole Auger-Richard, my forever patient French teacher, for double-checking my French and for her translation of *"Prendre Un P'tit Coup"*; to the talented storyteller and musician Jennifer Armstrong for inspiring Caitlin's "marry yourself" exercise; to Gretchen and Bill Straub and their amazing pumpkin, "Godzilla"; and to our neighbors, Carmen and Doug Burnell, for telling me the story of how they met, which became "Partial to Pickles." I learned Caitlin's perspective exercise from Ken Nelson at Kripalu. I don't know where he got it, but thanks, Ken!

Thank you to Amber Dahlin for her invaluable feedback on "The Moose in Me" speech. To Liz Korabek-Emerson for the "service work" idea, and for being such a true and trusted friend. And to the wonderful women in my writers' group back then, Tess Feltes, Kathy Gunst, Marie Harris, Pat Spalding, and Mimi White—I appreciate your astute feedback and encouragement.

Dean Lunt and Amy Canfield, thank you for seeking me out, and for your faith that I could write this book. Special thanks for your careful editing and encouragement. And to all the folks at Islandport Press, for believing in Ida and this book. Becky Rule, thanks so much for writing the foreword, and for being such a great supporter (and wicked talented writer and storyteller, to boot!).

I want to thank the Carlisles for welcoming Ida and me into your family, and for your continued love and support. A special thanks goes to Robert, whose dedication and discipline as a writer continues to inspire me.

To the great State of Maine, I am in love with you. I miss you when I'm gone! After three days, I get homesick. I mean, my heart actually aches. I miss the way the trees look by the lake, the rocky coastline, the mountains, and the long, flat stretches of road. Most of all, I miss the Maineiacs who call this neck of the woods home.

And to all Ida's fans, thanks for the laughter, loyalty, and encouragement. Ida and I just couldn't do it without you!

Finally, a heartfelt thanks to my best reader, friend, and husband, Gordon Carlisle, for your patient editing and insightful feedback.

I thank you, all!

Susan Poulin
May 2020